RESTful Web API Des
Node.js

Second Edition

Design and implement efficient RESTful solutions with this practical hands-on guide

Valentin Bojinov

BIRMINGHAM - MUMBAI

RESTful Web API Design with Node.js

Second Edition

Copyright © 2016 Packt Publishing

All rights reserved. No part of this book may be reproduced, stored in a retrieval system, or transmitted in any form or by any means, without the prior written permission of the publisher, except in the case of brief quotations embedded in critical articles or reviews.

Every effort has been made in the preparation of this book to ensure the accuracy of the information presented. However, the information contained in this book is sold without warranty, either express or implied. Neither the author, nor Packt Publishing, and its dealers and distributors will be held liable for any damages caused or alleged to be caused directly or indirectly by this book.

Packt Publishing has endeavored to provide trademark information about all of the companies and products mentioned in this book by the appropriate use of capitals. However, Packt Publishing cannot guarantee the accuracy of this information.

First published: March 2015

Second edition: May 2016

Production reference: 1200516

Published by Packt Publishing Ltd.

Livery Place

35 Livery Street

Birmingham B32PB, UK.

ISBN 978-1-78646-913-7

www.packtpub.com

Credits

Author

Valentin Bojinov

Reviewer

Huseyin BABAL

Commissioning Editor

Amarabha Banerjee

Acquisition Editor

Reshma Raman

Content Development Editor

Shali Deeraj

Technical Editor

Prajakta Mhatre

Copy Editor

Charlotte Carneiro

Project Coordinator

Sanchita Mandal

Proofreader

Safis Editing

Indexer

Hemangini Bari

Production Coordinator

Melwyn D'sa

Cover Work

Melwyn D'sa

About the Author

Valentin Bojinov studied computer programming at the Technological School of Electronic Systems in Sofia, Bulgaria, a college within the Technical University of Sofia. He was introduced to programming there and realized that his career would be in research and development. He holds a BSc in telecommunication and information engineering. Then, his interest in data transmission grew, and he ventured into B2B (business-to-business) communication. He is currently pursuing his MSc in software development. Valentin is an expert in Java, SOAP, RESTful web services, and B2B integration.

A few years after he started his career as a .NET developer, he realized that B2B and SOA were his passion. He then moved to SAP, where he contributed to the development of the web services stack of the SAP JEE platform. He currently works as a senior Java developer for the Bulgarian branch of Seeburger AG, a leader in the B2B and MFT solutions market. There, he develops and maintains several B2B communication adapters, including web services and SAP adapters.

I would like to take the opportunity to thank my soulmate Galya for putting up with me and with my decision to work on this title. Also, many thanks to my lovely parents, my dad Emil for encouraging me to study computers 20 years ago, and to mummy Anka for always being there for me! Special thanks to all my mentors from TUES for showing me how to learn efficiently and to never give up, the credit here goes mainly to Lubomir Chorbadjiev. I also have to mention my extraordinary colleagues I had the chance to study with! Guys, thanks for always being such good friends and experts! I know I haven't recently shown on our regular monthly gathering, so next time beer is on me!

About the Reviewer

Huseyin BABAL is an enthusiast full stack developer since 2007 who mainly develops web applications by using Java, Node.js and PHP on the backend; AngularJS and Twitter Bootstrap on the frontend; and Elasticsearch and MongoDB for some research projects. He is the author of *Node.js in Action* on Udemy with 1500+ students. He is also interested in DevOps engineering and applies continuous delivery principles to his projects. He writes tutorials about full stack development on Tuts+ and Java Code Geeks and shares his experiences at public conferences.

Besides the computer world, he lives in Istanbul with his wonderful wife and two cockatiels. He likes to spend his spare time with his wife by walking at least 1 hour per day, visiting different places, watching cartoons, and going on summer holidays.

www.PacktPub.com

eBooks, discount offers, and more

Did you know that Packt offers eBook versions of every book published, with PDF and ePub files available? You can upgrade to the eBook version at www.PacktPub.com and as a print book customer, you are entitled to a discount on the eBook copy. Get in touch with us at customercare@packtpub.com for more details.

At www.PacktPub.com, you can also read a collection of free technical articles, sign up for a range of free newsletters and receive exclusive discounts and offers on Packt books and eBooks.

https://www2.packtpub.com/books/subscription/packtlib

Do you need instant solutions to your IT questions? PacktLib is Packt's online digital book library. Here, you can search, access, and read Packt's entire library of books.

Why subscribe?

- Fully searchable across every book published by Packt
- Copy and paste, print, and bookmark content
- On demand and accessible via a web browser

Table of Contents

Preface

RESTful services have become the de facto standard data feed providers for social services, news feeds, and mobile devices. They deliver a large amount of data to millions of users; therefore, they need to address high-availability requirements such as reliability and scalability. This book will show you how to utilize the Node.js platform to implement a robust and performant data service. By the end of the book you will have learned how to implement a real-life RESTful service, taking advantage of the modern NoSQL database for serving both JSON and binary content. Important topics such as correct URI structuring and security features are also covered with detailed examples, showing you everything you need to know to start implementing robust RESTful APIs serving content for your applications!

What this book covers

Chapter 1, *REST – What You Did Not Know*, gives you a brief introduction into the history of REST and how it couples with the HTTP protocol.

Chapter 2, *Getting Started with Node.js*, teaches you how to install Node.js and how to work with its package manager to install modules, develop your first HTTP server application, and write automated unit tests for the HTTP handler by using mock request objects.

Chapter 3, *Building a Typical Web API*, teaches you how to structure your application using human-readable URL and URI parameters and develop a read-only RESTful service application using the filesystem as storage.

Chapter 4, *Using NoSQL Databases*, explains how to use LevelDB and MongoDB NoSQL databases, understand the difference between key/value and document data stores, and write automated tests for NoSQL user defined modules.

Chapter 5, *Implementing a Full-Fledged RESTful Service*, implements a production-ready RESTful service that uses NoSQL to store its data. You will also learn how to handle binary data and how to version an API while it evolves.

Chapter 6, *Keeping the Bad Guys Out*, explains how to restrict access to your data by choosing an appropriate authentication approach, protect data leakage with transport layer security.

What you need for this book

The following software is required to test the code present in this book:

- Node.js
- Enide developer studio or the Nodeclipse plugin for the Eclipse IDE
- SoapUI
- OpenSSL

Who this book is for

This book targets developers who want to enrich their development skills by learning how to develop scalable, server-side, RESTful applications based on the Node.js platform. You also need to be aware of HTTP communication concepts and should have a working knowledge of the JavaScript language. Knowledge of REST would be an added advantage but is definitely not a necessity.

Conventions

In this book, you will find a number of text styles that distinguish between different kinds of information. Here are some examples of these styles and an explanation of their meaning.

Code words in text, database table names, folder names, filenames, file extensions, pathnames, dummy URLs, user input, and Twitter handles are shown as follows: "All Node.js modules contain a `package.json` descriptor file."

A block of code is set as follows:

```
"dependencies": {
    "url": "0.1.x",
    "express": "4.7.x"
}
```

Any command-line input or output is written as follows:

```
nodeunit test-math.js
```

New terms and **important words** are shown in bold. Words that you see on the screen, for example, in menus or dialog boxes, appear in the text like this: "Let's start by creating a workspace in Enide Studio. Navigate to **File** | **New** | **Node.js Project** and enter the name of your first project."

Warnings or important notes appear in a box like this.

Tips and tricks appear like this.

Reader feedback

Feedback from our readers is always welcome. Let us know what you think about this book-what you liked or disliked. Reader feedback is important for us as it helps us develop titles that you will really get the most out of. To send us general feedback, simply e-mail feedback@packtpub.com, and mention the book's title in the subject of your message. If there is a topic that you have expertise in and you are interested in either writing or contributing to a book, see our author guide at www.packtpub.com/authors.

Customer support

Now that you are the proud owner of a Packt book, we have a number of things to help you to get the most from your purchase.

Downloading the example code

You can download the example code files for this book from your account at http://www.packtpub.com. If you purchased this book elsewhere, you can visit http://www.packtpub.com/support and register to have the files e-mailed directly to you.

You can download the code files by following these steps:

1. Log in or register to our website using your e-mail address and password.
2. Hover the mouse pointer on the **SUPPORT** tab at the top.
3. Click on **Code Downloads & Errata**.

4. Enter the name of the book in the **Search** box.
5. Select the book for which you're looking to download the code files.
6. Choose from the drop-down menu where you purchased this book from.
7. Click on **Code Download**.

You can also download the code files by clicking on the **Code Files** button on the book's webpage at the Packt Publishing website. This page can be accessed by entering the book's name in the **Search** box. Please note that you need to be logged into your Packt account. Once the file is downloaded, please make sure that you unzip or extract the folder using the latest version of:

- WinRAR / 7-Zip for Windows
- Zipeg / iZip / UnRarX for Mac
- 7-Zip / PeaZip for Linux

The code bundle for the book is also hosted on GitHub at `https://github.com/PacktPu blishing/RESTful-Web-API-Design-with-Node.JS-Second-Edition/tree/maste r`. We also have other code bundles from our rich catalog of books and videos available at `h ttps://github.com/PacktPublishing/`. Check them out!

Errata

Although we have taken every care to ensure the accuracy of our content, mistakes do happen. If you find a mistake in one of our books-maybe a mistake in the text or the code-we would be grateful if you could report this to us. By doing so, you can save other readers from frustration and help us improve subsequent versions of this book. If you find any errata, please report them by visiting `http://www.packtpub.com/submit-errata`, selecting your book, clicking on the **Errata Submission Form** link, and entering the details of your errata. Once your errata are verified, your submission will be accepted and the errata will be uploaded to our website or added to any list of existing errata under the Errata section of that title.

To view the previously submitted errata, go to `https://www.packtpub.com/books/con tent/support` and enter the name of the book in the search field. The required information will appear under the **Errata** section.

Piracy

Piracy of copyrighted material on the Internet is an ongoing problem across all media. At Packt, we take the protection of our copyright and licenses very seriously. If you come across any illegal copies of our works in any form on the Internet, please provide us with the location address or website name immediately so that we can pursue a remedy.

Please contact us at `copyright@packtpub.com` with a link to the suspected pirated material.

We appreciate your help in protecting our authors and our ability to bring you valuable content.

Questions

If you have a problem with any aspect of this book, you can contact us at `questions@packtpub.com`, and we will do our best to address the problem.

1
REST – What You Did Not Know

Nowadays, topics such as cloud computing and mobile device service feeds, as well as other data sources driven by cutting-edge, scalable, stateless, and modern technologies such as RESTful web services, leave the impression that REST was invented recently. Well, to be honest, it definitely was not! In fact, REST has been here since the end of the 20th century.

This chapter will walk you through REST's fundamental principles, and it will explain how REST couples with the HTTP protocol. You will look into the five key principles that need to be considered while turning an HTTP application into a RESTful-service-enabled application. You will also look at the differences in describing RESTful and classic SOAP-based web services. Finally, you will learn how to utilize already existing infrastructure for your benefit.

In this chapter, we will cover the following topics:

- REST fundamentals
- REST with HTTP
- Essential differences in the description and discovery of RESTful services compared to classical SOAP-based services
- Taking advantage of existing infrastructure

REST fundamentals

It actually happened back in 1999, when a request for comments was submitted to the **Internet Engineering Task Force (IETF**: http://www.ietf.org/) via RFC 2616: "Hypertext Transfer Protocol-HTTP/1.1." One of its authors, Roy Fielding, later defined a set of principles built around the HTTP and URI standards. This gave birth to REST as we know it today.

 These definitions were given in Chapter 5, *Representational State Transfer (REST)*, of Fielding's dissertation called *Architectural Styles and the Design of Network-based Software Architectures*. The dissertation is still available at http://www.ics.uci.edu/~fielding/pubs/dissertation/rest_a rch_style.htm.

Let's look at the key principles around the HTTP and URI standards, sticking to which will make your HTTP application a RESTful-service-enabled application:

- Everything is a resource
- Each resource is identifiable by a unique identifier (URI)
- Use the standard HTTP methods
- Resources can have multiple representations
- Communicate statelessly

Principle 1 – everything is a resource

To understand this principle, one must conceive the idea of representing data by a specific format and not by a physical file. Each piece of data available on the Internet has a format that could be described by a content type. For example, JPEG images; MPEG videos; HTML, XML, and text documents; and binary data are all resources with the following content types: image/jpeg, video/mpeg, text/html, text/xml, and application/octet-stream.

Principle 2 – each resource is identifiable by a unique identifier

Since the Internet contains so many different resources, they all should be accessible via URIs and should be identified uniquely. Furthermore, the URIs can be in a human-readable format, despite the fact that their consumers are more likely to be software programs rather than ordinary humans.

Human-readable URIs keep data self-descriptive and ease further development against it. This helps you to reduce the risk of logical errors in your programs to a minimum.

Here are a few sample examples of such URIs:

- `http://www.mydatastore.com/images/vacation/2014/summer`
- `http://www.mydatastore.com/videos/vacation/2014/winter`
- `http://www.mydatastore.com/data/documents/balance?format=xml`
- `http://www.mydatastore.com/data/archives/2014`

These human-readable URIs expose different types of resources in a straightforward manner. In the example, it is quite clear that the media types of these resources are as follows:

- Images
- Videos
- XML documents
- Some kinds of binary archive documents

Principle 3 – use the standard HTTP methods

The native HTTP protocol (RFC 2616) defines eight actions, also known as HTTP verbs:

- `GET`
- `POST`
- `PUT`
- `DELETE`
- `HEAD`
- `OPTIONS`

- TRACE
- CONNECT

The first four of them feel just natural in the context of resources, especially when defining actions for resource data manipulation. Let's make a parallel with relative SQL databases where the native language for data manipulation is **CRUD** (short for **Create, Read, Update, and Delete**) originating from the different types of SQL statements: INSERT, SELECT, UPDATE, and DELETE, respectively. In the same manner, if you apply the REST principles correctly, the HTTP verbs should be used as shown here:

HTTP verb	Action	Response status code
GET	Requests an existing resource	"200 OK" if the resource exists, "404 Not Found" if it does not exist, and "500 Internal Server Error" for other errors
PUT	Updates a resource or creates it as an identifier provided from the client	"201 CREATED" if a new resource is created, "200 OK" if updated, and "500 Internal Server Error" for other errors
POST	Creates a resource with an identifier generated at server side or updates a resource with an existing identifier provided from the client	"201 CREATED" if a new resource is created,"200 OK" if the resource has been updated successfully, "404 Not Found" if the resource to be updated does not exist, and "500 Internal Server Error" for other errors
DELETE	Deletes a resource	"200 OK"or "204 No Content" if the resource has been deleted successfully, "404 Not Found" if the resource to be deleted does not exist, and "500 Internal Server Error" for other errors

Note that a resource can be created by either of POST or PUT HTTP verbs. When a resource has to be created under a specific URI with an identifier provided by the client, then PUT is the appropriate action:

```
PUT /data/documents/balance/22082014 HTTP/1.1
Content-Type: text/xml
Host: www.mydatastore.com

<?xml version="1.0" encoding="utf-8"?>
<balance date="22082014">
```

```
<Item>Sample item</Item>
<price currency="EUR">100</price>
</balance>

HTTP/1.1 201 Created
Content-Type: text/xml
Location: /data/documents/balance/22082014
```

However, in your application, you may want to leave it up to the server REST application to decide where to place the newly created resource, and thus create it under an appropriate but still unknown or non-existing location.

For instance, in our example, we might want the server to create the date part of the URI based on the current date. In such cases, it is perfectly fine to use the POST verb to the main resource URI and let the server respond with the location of the newly created resource:

```
POST /data/documents/balance HTTP/1.1
Content-Type: text/xml
Host: www.mydatastore.com

<?xml version="1.0" encoding="utf-8"?>
<balance date="22082014">
<Item>Sample item</Item>
<price currency="EUR">100</price>
</balance>

HTTP/1.1 201 Created
Content-Type: text/xml
Location: /data/documents/balance
```

Principle 4 – resources can have multiple representations

A key feature of a resource is that it may be represented in a different form than the one it is stored. Thus, it can be requested or posted in different representations. As long as the specified format is supported, the REST-enabled endpoint should use it. In the preceding example, we posted an XML representation of a balance, but if the server supported the JSON format, the following request would have been valid as well:

```
POST /data/documents/balance HTTP/1.1
Content-Type: application/json
Host: www.mydatastore.com

{
```

```
    "balance": {
      "date": ""22082014"",
      "Item": "Sample item",
      "price": {
        "-currency": "EUR",
        "#text": "100"
      }
    }
  }
}
HTTP/1.1 201 Created
Content-Type: application/json
Location: /data/documents/balance
```

Principle 5 – communicate statelessly

Resource manipulation operations through HTTP requests should always be considered atomic. All modifications of a resource should be carried out within an HTTP request in isolation. After the request execution, the resource is left in a final state, which implicitly means that partial resource updates are not supported. You should always send the complete state of the resource.

Back to the balance example, updating the price field of a given balance would mean posting a complete JSON document that contains all of the balance data, including the updated price field. Posting only the updated price is not stateless, as it implies that the application is aware that the resource has a price field, that is, it knows its state.

Another requirement for your RESTful application is to be stateless; the fact that once deployed in a production environment, it is likely that incoming requests are served by a load balancer, ensuring scalability and high availability. Once exposed via a load balancer, the idea of keeping your application state at server side gets compromised. This doesn't mean that you are not allowed to keep the state of your application. It just means that you should keep it in a RESTful way. For example, keep a part of the state within the URI.

The statelessness of your RESTful API isolates the caller against changes at the server side. Thus, the caller is not expected to communicate with the same server in consecutive requests. This allows easy application of changes within the server infrastructure, such as adding or removing nodes.

 Remember that it is your responsibility to keep your RESTful APIs stateless, as the consumers of the API would expect it to be.

Now that you know that REST is around 15 years old, a sensible question would be, "why has it become so popular just quite recently?" My answer to the question is that we as developers usually reject simple, straightforward approaches, and most of the time, prefer spending more time on turning already complex solutions into even more complex and sophisticated ones.

Take classical SOAP web services for example. Their various WS-* specifications are so many and sometimes so loosely defined, that in order to make different solutions from different vendors interoperable, a separate specification WS-Basic Profile has been introduced.It defines extra interoperability rules in order to ensure that all WS-* specifications in SOAP-based web services can work together.

When it comes to transporting binary data with classical web services over HTTP, things get even more complex—as SOAP-based web services provide different ways of transporting binary data. Each way is defined in other sets of specifications such as SOAP with **Attachment References (SwaRef)** and **Message Transmission Optimization Mechanism (MTOM).** All this complexity was caused mainly because the initial idea of the web service was to execute business logic remotely, not to transport large amounts of data.

Well, I personally think that when it comes to data transfer, things should not be that complex. This is where REST comes into play, by introducing the concept of resources and a standard means for manipulating them.

The REST goals

Now that we've covered the main REST principles, let's dive deeper into what can be achieved when they are followed:

- Separation of the representation and the resource
- Visibility
- Reliability
- Scalability
- Performance

Separation of the representation and the resource

A resource is just a set of information, and as defined by *Principle 4*, it can have multiple representations; however, its state is atomic. It is up to the caller to specify the desired media type with the accept header in the HTTP request, and then it is up to the server application to handle the representation accordingly and return the appropriate content type of the resource and a relevant HTTP status code:

- `HTTP 200 OK` in the case of success
- `HTTP 400 Bad Request` if an unsupported content type is requested or for any other invalid request

- `HTTP 500 Internal Server Error` when something unexpected happens during the request processing

For instance, let's assume that at server side, we have balance resources stored in an XML format. We can have an API that allows a consumer to request the resource in various formats, such as `application/json`, `application/zip`, `application/octet-stream`, and so on.

It would be up to the API itself to load the requested resource, transform it into the requested type (for example, JSON or XML), and either use ZIP to compress it or directly flush it to the HTTP response output.

The caller can make use of the `Accept` HTTP header to specify the expected media type of the response data. So, if we want to request our balance data inserted in the previous section in XML format, the following request should be executed:

```
GET /data/balance/22082014 HTTP/1.1
Host: my-computer-hostname
Accept: text/xml

HTTP/1.1 200 OK
Content-Type: text/xml
Content-Length: 140

<?xml version="1.0" encoding="utf-8"?>
<balance date="22082014">
<Item>Sample item</Item>
<price currency="EUR">100</price>
</balance>
```

To request the same balance in JSON format, the `Accept` header needs to be set to `application/json`:

```
GET /data/balance/22082014 HTTP/1.1
Host: my-computer-hostname
Accept: application/json

HTTP/1.1 200 OK
Content-Type: application/json
Content-Length: 120

{
"balance": {
"date": "22082014",
"Item": "Sample item",
"price": {
"-currency": "EUR",
"#text": "100"
    }
  }
}
```

Visibility

REST is designed to be visible and simple. Visibility of the service means that every aspect of it should self-descriptive and follow the natural HTTP language according to principles 3, 4, and 5.

Visibility in the context of the outer world would mean that monitoring applications would be interested only in the HTTP communication between the REST service and the caller. Since the requests and responses are stateless and atomic, nothing more is needed to flow the behavior of the application and to understand whether anything has gone wrong.

Remember that caching reduces the visibility of your restful applications and in general should be avoided, unless needed for serving resources subject to large amounts of callers. In such cases, caching may be an option, after carefully evaluating the possible consequences of serving obsolete data.

Reliability

Before talking about reliability, we need to define which HTTP methods are safe and which are idempotent in the REST context. So, let's first define what safe and idempotent methods are:

- An HTTP method is considered to be safe provided that when requested, it does not modify or cause any side effects on the state of the resource
- An HTTP method is considered to be idempotent if its response is always the same, no matter how many times it is requested

The following table lists shows you which HTTP method is safe and which is idempotent:

HTTP Method	Safe	Idempotent
GET	Yes	Yes
POST	No	No
PUT	No	Yes
DELETE	No	Yes

Scalability and performance

So far, I have often stressed the importance of having stateless implementation and stateless behavior for a RESTful web application. The **World Wide Web** (**WWW**) is an enormous universe, containing a huge amount of data and a lot of users eager to get that data. The evolution of the WWW has brought the requirement that applications should scale easily as their load increases. Scaling applications that have a state is hardly possible, especially when zero or close-to-zero downtime is needed.

That's why being stateless is crucial for any application that needs to scale. In the best-case scenario, scaling your application would require you to put another piece of hardware for a load balancer. There would be no need for the different nodes to sync between each other, as they should not care about the state at all. Scalability is all about serving all your clients in an acceptable amount of time. Its main idea is to keep your application running and to prevent **Denial of Service** (**DoS**) caused by a huge amount of incoming requests.

Scalability should not be confused with performance of an application. Performance is measured by the time needed for a single request to be processed, not by the total number of requests that the application can handle. The asynchronous non-blocking architecture and event-driven design of Node.js make it a logical choice for implementing an application that scales and performs well.

Working with WADL

If you are familiar with SOAP web services, you may have heard of the **Web Service Definition Language** (**WSDL**). It is an XML description of the interface of the service and defines an endpoint URL for invocation. It is mandatory for a SOAP web service to be described by such a WSDL definition.

Similar to SOAP web services, RESTful services can also make use of a description language, called WADL. **WADL** stands for **Web Application Definition Language**. Unlike WSDL for SOAP web services, a WADL description of a RESTful service is optional, that is, consuming the service has nothing to do with its description.

Here is a sample part of a WADL file that describes the GET operation of our balance service:

```
<application xmlns="http://wadl.dev.java.net/2009/02"
xmlns:xsd="http://www.w3.org/2001/XMLSchema"
xmlns:service="http://localhost:8080/data/balance">
<grammer>
<include href="balance.xsd"/>
<include href="error.xsd"/>
</grammer>
<resources base="http://localhost:8080/data/balance/">
<resource path="{date}">
<method name="GET">
<request>
<param name="date" type="xsd:string" style="template"/>
</request>
<response status="200">
<representation mediaType="application/xml" element="service:balance"/>
<representation mediaType="application/json" />
</response>
<response status="404">
<representation mediaType="application/xml" element="service:balance"/>
</response>
</method>
```

```
</resource>
</resources>
</application>
```

This extract of a WADL file shows how application-exposing resources are described. Basically, each resource must be a part of an application. The resource provides the URI where it is located with the base attribute, and describes each of its supported HTTP methods in a method. Additionally, an optional doc element can be used at resource and application to provide additional documentation about the service and its operations.

Though WADL is optional, it significantly reduces the efforts of discovering RESTful services.

Taking advantage of the existing infrastructure

The best part of developing and distributing RESTful applications is that the infrastructure needed is already out there waiting restlessly for you. As RESTful applications use the existing web space heavily, you need to do nothing more than follow the REST principles when developing. In addition, there are plenty of libraries available out there for any platform, and I do mean any given platform. This eases development of RESTful applications, so you just need to choose the preferred platform for you and start developing.

Summary

In this chapter, you learned about foundation of a REST, looking at the five key principles that turn a web application into a REST-enabled application. We made a slight comparison between RESTful services and classical SOAP web services, and finally took a look at how RESTful services are described and how we can simplify the discovery of the services we develop.

Now that you know the basics, we are ready to dive into the Node.js way of implementing RESTful services. In the next chapter, you will learn about the essentials of Node.js and the accompanying tools that are necessary to use and understand in order to build a real-life fully-fledged web service.

2
Getting Started with Node.js

In this chapter, you will gain your first real experience with Node.js. We will start by installing Node.js, along with some of the modules we will use throughout this book. Then, we will set up a development environment. I have chosen the Nodeclipse plugin for the well-known Eclipse IDE, which comes preinstalled within the Enide Developer Studio.

Next, we will create a workspace and start developing our first Node.js application. It will be a simple server processing incoming HTTP requests. Then we will go one step further, demonstrating how to modularize and test our JavaScript code. Finally, we will take a look at some cloud environment offerings that we can use to deploy our applications.

To sum up, in this chapter, we will cover the following topics:

- Installing Node.js
- Installing the Express framework and other modules
- Setting up a development environment
- Handling HTTP requests
- Modularizing code
- Testing Node.js
- Deploying an application on a cloud environment

Installing Node.js

The current version of the latest Node.js release is five. This is a stable short-term support release, which should serve as a bridge between the latest *Long Term Support* and the following one.

Let's start our journey through Node.js with a Node.js installation. Installers are available both for Windows and Mac operating systems at `http://www.nodejs.org/download/`. Linux users can either build Node.js from the available Linux binaries or can make use of their package manager, as Node.js is available with most of the popular package repositories for different Linux distributions. Currently, there are two versions available in the repositoriesâ©ï¸the LTS Version 4.x and the stable 5.x. By default, the package manager points to the LTS release, so we should explicitly tell the manager to install the 5.x Version via the following command:

```
curl -sL https://deb.nodesource.com/setup_5.x | sudo -E bash -
apt-get install nodejs
```

For now, let's install Node.js from its installer. A wizard will guide you through a rather usual installation procedure where you will have to accept the Node.js license agreement and then provide an installation path.

The installer will have preselected for you the Node.js runtime, NPM , shortcuts to online documentation resources, the option to add Node.js, and the NPM package manager to your operating system `PATH` environment variable, as shown in the following screenshot:

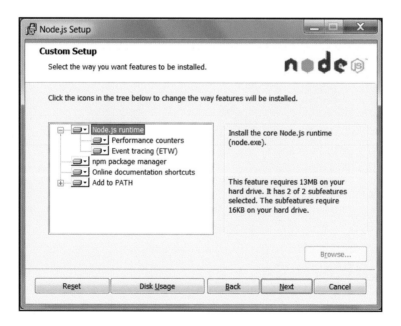

Linux users performing installations via package managers will need to install the NPM package manager separately. After a successful installation, you should have `node` set on your `PATH` environment variable. Test whether `node` is installed correctly by executing the following command:

```
node -version
```

 At the time of writing this book, the latest Node.js version is v5.5.0; so as expected, this version number will be the output of the version check.

Node Package Manager

Node.js eases support to third-party open source developed modules by providing the **Node Package Manager** (we've already mentioned it, that is, **NPM**). It allows you, as a developer, to easily install, manage, and even provide your own modules for a rapidly grown and well-maintained open source repository. It is available at `http://www.npmjs.org/` and is accessible via its command-line interface.

If you didn't use the installer, then you will need to install NPM separately. For example, Ubuntu users can make use of their package installer as follows:

```
apt-get npm install
```

Once NPM is installed, you may want to set it permanently in your user profile's `PATH` environment variable by editing the `~/.profile` file to export the path to NPM as follows:

```
export PATH=$PATH:/path/to/npm
```

After a successful NPM installation, use NPM's `ls` option to display the already installed Node.js modules:

```
valio@G771JW:~/workspace/chapter2$ npm ls
chapter2@0.0.0 /home/valio/workspace/chapter2
├─┬ body-parser@1.13.3
│ ├── bytes@2.1.0
│ ├── content-type@1.0.1
│ ├─┬ debug@2.2.0
│ │ └── ms@0.7.1
│ ├── depd@1.0.1
│ ├─┬ http-errors@1.3.1
│ │ ├── inherits@2.0.1
│ │ └── statuses@1.2.1
│ ├── iconv-lite@0.4.11
│ ├─┬ on-finished@2.3.0
│ │ └── ee-first@1.1.1
│ ├── qs@4.0.0
│ ├─┬ raw-body@2.1.5
│ │ ├── bytes@2.2.0
│ │ ├── iconv-lite@0.4.13
│ │ └── unpipe@1.0.0
│ └─┬ type-is@1.6.11
│   ├── media-typer@0.3.0
│   └─┬ mime-types@2.1.10
│     └── mime-db@1.22.0
├─┬ cookie-parser@1.3.5
```

Installing the Express framework and other modules

Now that we have NPM installed, let's make use of it and install some of the modules that we will be using heavily throughout this book. The most important among them is the Express framework (http://www.expressjs.com/). It is a flexible web applicationframework for Node.js, providing a robust RESTful API for provisioning data to single or multipage web applications. The following command will download the Express module from the https://www.npmjs.com/ repository and will make it available for our local node installation:

```
npm install express -g
```

After a successful installation of the module, it will be among the results of an `npm ls` output. Later in this chapter, we will take a look at how to write unit tests for our Node.js modules. So, we also need to install the `nodeunit` module:

```
npm install nodeunit -g
```

The −g option will install the module globally. This means that the module will be stored according to your Node.js's global configuration. Globally installed modules are available to all Node.js applications. If a local installation is carried out, the modules will be stored in a `node_modules` subdirectory of the current working directory of your project and will be available only to that directory.

Coming back to the Nodeunit module, it provides basic assert test functions for creating unit tests as well as tools for executing them.

Now that we have seen how to install modules, there is one more thing to look at before starting to develop Node.js code. That is the package descriptor file of Node.js modules.

All Node.js modules contain a `package.json` descriptor file. It provides meta information about the module itself. Let's take a look at the `package.json` file of the Nodeunit we just installed:

```json
{
    "name": "nodeunit",
    "version": "0.9.1",
    "description": "Easy unit testing for node.js and the
     browser.",
    "maintainers": [
        {
            "name": "Caolan McMahon",
            "web": "https://github.com/caolan"
        }
    ],
    "contributors": [
        {
            "name": "Romain Beauxis",
            "web": "https://github.com/toots"
        }
    ],
    "repository": {
        "type": "git",
        "url": "http://github.com/caolan/nodeunit.git"
    },
    "devDependencies": {
        "uglify-js": ">=1.1.0",
        "should": ">=0.4.2"
    },
    "bugs": {
        "url": "http://github.com/caolan/nodeunit/issues"
    },
    "licenses": [
        {
```

```
      "type": "MIT",
      "url": "http://github.com/caolan/nodeunit/raw/master
      /LICENSE"
    }
  ],
  "directories": {
    "lib": "./lib",
    "doc": "./doc",
    "man": "./man1"
  },
  "bin": {
    "nodeunit": "./bin/nodeunit"
  },
  "dependencies": {
    "tap": "^0.7.1"
  },
  "scripts": {
    "test": "node ./bin/nodeunit"
  }
}
```

Downloading the example code

Code Detailed steps to download the code bundle are mentioned in the `Preface` of this book.

The code bundle for the book is also hosted on GitHub at `https://githu` `b.com/PacktPublishing/RESTful-Web-API-Design-with-Node.JS` `-Second-Edition/tree/master`. We also have other code bundles from our rich catalog of books and videos available at `https://github.com/P` `acktPublishing/`. Check them out!

The name and the version of the package are mandatory properties for every module. All other pieces of metainformation, such as the contributors list, repository type and location, license information, and others are optional. One of the most interesting properties that is worth mentioning is the `dependencies` property. It tells NPM which are the modules that your package depends on.

Let's take a deeper look at how this is specified. Assume we have the following structure for the `dependencies` JSON:

```
"dependencies": {
    "url": "0.1.x",
    "express": "4.7.x"
}
```

This tells NPM that our package depends on the `url` and `express` modules. Furthermore, it specifies the versions for those dependencies. So when NPM installs the module, it will implicitly download and install the latest minor versions of the `url` and `express` modules.

You have the options to define, strictly, the version of a dependency by specifying it in the following format: `major.minor.patch-version`. In our previous example, the dependencies JSON will tell NPM to download the latest patch of Version 0.1 of the `url` module as well as the latest patch version 4.7 for `express`. According to Node.js's best development practices, you should not have a major version specified with "`*`", because when modules evolve in major versions, they might lose their backward compatibility.

 For more information on versioning, visit the website of semantic versioning specification at `http://www.semver.org/`.`compatibility`.

NPM can be used to generate a `package.json` file for your application. Execute NPM install from your application directory, and NPM will ask you a couple of questions for your application and will gather the modules it uses. As a result you will have a `package.json` file generated and ready to use; it might require only slight adjustments as your application evolves.

Setting up a development environment

One thing that I truly miss when writing JavaScript code is a convenient and fully functional IDE with reasonable debugging capabilities. This is mainly related to the fact that most of the JavaScript code written is usually related to web frontend. This is definitely not the case when server-side JavaScript code, such as Node.js, is produced. Thus, development tools here can be much more unified, integrated, and easy to use.

The Nodeclipse project available at `http://www.nodeclipse.org/` is all about having a fully functional JavaScript IDE, including long-awaited features such as code completion, a convenient debugger, and a runtime inspector. All of these are integrated in the Eclipse environment, which already provides out-of-the-box integration with source code repositories and other infrastructural components.

You can choose to download the Node.js tool from the update site at `http://www.nodecl ipse.org/updates` or use the Enide Studio, which comes with all of the required development content preinstalled. It is available at `http://www.nodeclipse.org/enide/studio/`. I will use Enide Studio throughout this book.

Let's start by creating a workspace in Enide Studio. Navigate to **File** | **New** | **Node.js Project** and enter the name of your first project. You are now ready to start with Node.js. Now that we have a project, let's create our first Node.js application. Then, add the following new JavaScript source file named `hello-node.js` to the project:

```
var http = require('http');
var port = 8180;

function handle_request(request, response) {
    response.writeHead(200, {
        'Content-Type' : 'text/plain'
    });

    response.end('Hello World. Are you restless to go
    restful?\n');
    console.log('hello-node.js was requested');
}

http.createServer(handle_request).listen(port, '127.0.0.1');

console.log('Started Node.js http server at http://127.0.0.1:' +  port);
```

The `hello-node.js` file uses Node.js's HTTP module to start listening for the incoming requests on port 8180. It will reply with static text content as a response to each request. In addition, a log entry will be displayed on the console for each request. Now, let's start our application and then request it from our web browser. To start the application, execute the following command from your command line:

```
node hello-node.js
```

This will start the application, and it will be ready to process incoming requests. Also make sure to try out the debugging functionality provided by Node.js and Nodeclipse. To start your Node application with the debugging feature enabled, use the `--debug` option of Node.js, as follows:

```
node --debug hello-node.js
```

Then, launch your `hello-node.js` file from Nodeclipse by right-clicking on it and selecting the **Debug As Node** application and all the debugging features you are so used to from Eclipse or any other IDE, such as breakpoints and inspecting variables. Actually, anything a functional debugger can offer you is available. Awesome, isn't it?

Handling HTTP requests

Now that we created our first Node.js request handler, let's move on. Currently, our server application behaves in the same way no matter what kind of HTTP request is being processed. Let's extend it in a way that it behaves more HTTP server-like and start differentiating the incoming requests based on their type, by implementing handler functions for each one of them.

Let's create a new `hello-node-http-server.js`, as follows:

```
var http = require('http');
var port = 8180;

function handle_GET_request(response) {
  response.writeHead(200, {
    'Content-Type' : 'text/plain'
  });
  response.end('Get action was requested');
}

function handle_POST_request(response) {
  response.writeHead(200, {
    'Content-Type' : 'text/plain'
  });
  response.end('Post action was requested');
}

function handle_PUT_request(response) {
  response.writeHead(200, {
    'Content-Type' : 'text/plain'
  });
  response.end('Put action was requested');
}

function handle_HEAD_request(response) {
  response.writeHead(200, {
    'Content-Type' : 'text/plain'
  });
  response.end('Head action was requested');
}

function handle_DELETE_request(response) {
  response.writeHead(200, {
    'Content-Type' : 'text/plain'
  });
  response.end('Delete action was requested');
}
```

```
function handle_bad_request(response) {
  response.writeHead(400, {
    'Content-Type' : 'text/plain'
  });
  response.end('Bad request');
}

function handle_request(request, response) {

  switch (request.method) {
    case 'GET':
      handle_GET_request(response);
      break;
    case 'POST':
      handle_POST_request(response);
      break;
    case 'PUT':
      handle_PUT_request(response);
      break;
    case 'DELETE':
      handle_DELETE_request(response);
      break;
    case 'HEAD':
      handle_HEAD_request(response);
      break;
    default:
      handle_bad_request(response);
      break;
  }
  console.log('Request processing ended');
}

http.createServer(handle_request).listen(port, '127.0.0.1');

console.log('Started Node.js http server at http://127.0.0.1:' +  port);
```

When you run this application, our HTTP server will handle all known HTTP requests. In case of a faulty request, it will gracefully respond with HTTP 400 BAD REQUEST status code.

To test that, let's make use of another nice plugin of the Enide Developer Studioâ◎◎the RESTClient tool. It allows us to send any kind of HTTP requests to an exposed endpoint, such as our newly created server with a POST request:

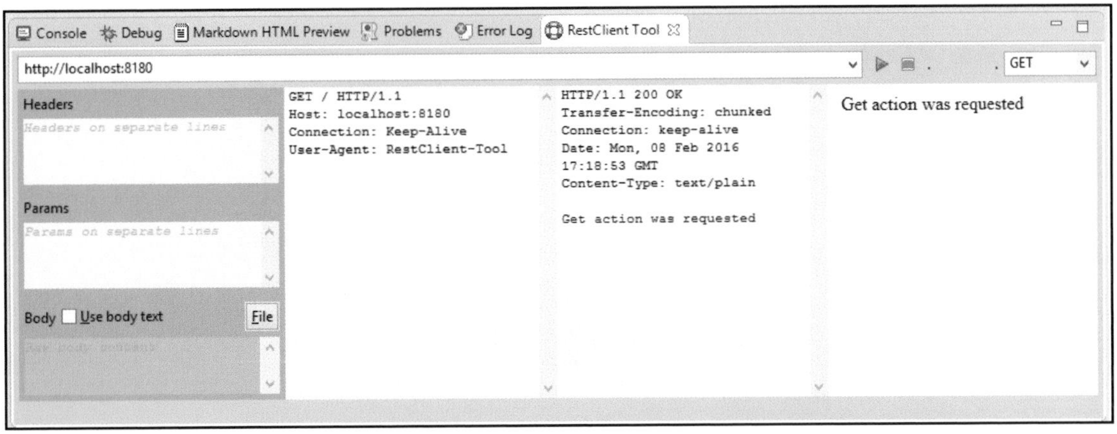

This plugin allows us to test HTTP endpoints with different requests and different payloads by allowing us to use files attached to the requests. Being integrated right into our development environment makes it the logical choice for our test tool for the upcoming development. Give it a try and execute test requests for each of the `handle` functions we implemented previously.

Modularizing code

What we developed so far is a simple HTTP server application that listens and processes known request types. However, it is obvious that our application is not well structured. We have one JavaScript server file that does all of the work for us. Node.js provides a variety of modules and additionally enables us to create modules of our own and reuse them in our application whenever necessary.

> A user-defined module is a logical unit consisting of one or more related functions. The module can export one or more functions to other components while keeping other functions visible only to itself.

We will rework our HTTP server application in a way that the entire request handling functionality will be wrapped into a module. This module will export only a generic handler function that will take the request as a parameter and, based on the request type, it will delegate the handling to inner functions.

Let's start by creating a new modules' directory within our project. We will refactor our previous source file by extracting the following functions to a new `http-module.js` file inside the newly created directory:

```
function handle_GET_request(request, response) {
  response.writeHead(200, {
    'Content-Type' : 'text/plain'
  });
  response.end('Get action was requested');
}

function handle_POST_request(request, response) {
  response.writeHead(200, {
    'Content-Type' : 'text/plain'
  });
  response.end('Post action was requested');
}

function handle_PUT_request(request, response) {
  response.writeHead(200, {
    'Content-Type' : 'text/plain'
  });
  response.end('Put action was requested');
}

function handle_HEAD_request(request, response) {
  response.writeHead(200, {
    'Content-Type' : 'text/plain'
  });
  response.end('Head action was requested');
}

function handle_DELETE_request(request, response) {
  response.writeHead(200, {
    'Content-Type' : 'text/plain'
  });
  response.end('Delete action was requested');
}

function handle_bad_request(request, response) {
  response.writeHead(400, {
    'Content-Type' : 'text/plain'
```

```
    });
    response.end('Bad request');
}

exports.handle_request = function (request, response) {

    switch (request.method) {
      case 'GET':
        handle_GET_request(request, response);
        break;
      case 'POST':
        handle_POST_request(request, response);
        break;
      case 'PUT':
        handle_PUT_request(request, response);
        break;
      case 'DELETE':
        handle_DELETE_request(request, response);
        break;
      case 'HEAD':
        handle_HEAD_request(request, response);
        break;
      default:
        handle_bad_request(request, response);
        break;
    }
    console.log('Request processing by http-module ended');
};
```

This file creates a user-defined module that exports the `handle_request` function to the outer components. All the other functions within the module are available only within the module. In our case, we export only one function, but basically, a module can export as many functions as is feasible.

Let's see how we can access our module from other Node.js files by creating the following new `main.js` file in the main directory of our first project:

```
var httpModule = require('./modules/http-module');

var http = require('http');
var port = 8080;

http.createServer(httpModule.handle_request).listen(port,   '127.0.0.1');
```

We separated the creation of the server socket and the business logic that handles the incoming requests. The `require` directive is used to import our module. It must use a relative path to it.

Execute another test with the RESTClient tool and with debugging enabled to test and debug the module we just created.

 Luckily, we will not be creating our own HTTP handlers when implementing our RESTful-enabled applications. The Express framework will do this for us. The examples in this chapter are meant to provide a clear example of the Node.js possibilities when it comes to handling HTTP requests and how user modules are implemented. We will take a detailed look at the Express framework in Chapter 3, *Building a Typical Web API*.

Testing Node.js

Now we will extend our project by providing a unit test for HTTP module, but before diving into that, first, let's see how Node.js supports unit testing in general. In the beginning of this chapter, we installed the Nodeunit module. Now it's about time we started playing around with it.

First, let's create another Node.js's simple module that we will use to implement our first unit test. Then, we will move to more advanced topics such as mocking JavaScript objects and use them to create unit tests for our HTTP module.

I have chosen to develop a simple math module that exports functions for adding and subtracting integer numbers, as it is straightforward enough and the results of each operation are strictly defined, as follows:

1. Let's start with the module and create the following math.js file in our module directory:

```
exports.add = function (x, y) {
  return x + y;
};
exports.subtract = function (x, y) {
  return x - y;
};
```

2. The next step will be to create a test-math.js file in the test subdirectory of our project:

```
var math = require('../modules/math');
exports.test_add = function (test) {
  test.equal(math.add(1, 1), 2);
  test.done();
};
```

```
exports.test_subtract = function (test) {
  test.equals(math.subtract(4,2), 2);
  test.done();
};
```

3. Finally, in order to run our newly created test, we open a command-line console and execute the following:

```
nodeunit test-math.js
```

4. The output will show all the results of all the test methods we exported together with information whether our test passed successfully or not:

```
test-math.js
? test_add
? test_subtract
OK: 2 assertions (8ms)
```

5. Let's change `test_add` in a way that it gets broken in order to see how test failure is reported by the Nodeunit module:

```
exports.test_add = function (test) {
    test.equal(math.add(1, 1), 3);
    test.done();
};
```

6. Then, we execute our test again. This time, we will see a failure ending with some assert failure messages, and in the end, we'll see an aggregation saying that some of the executed tests failed:

```
nodeunit test-math.js
(...)
FAILURES: 1/2 assertions failed (12ms)
```

We just created our Nodeunit's first unit test. However, it tests the `math` function in a rather isolated way. I suppose you are wondering how we can use Nodeunit, which takes complex parameters such as HTTP `request` and `response`, to test code as arguments. This is possible using so called **mock objects**. They are something like a snapshot version of the state of complex objects that we want to use in our unit test in order to test the behavior of our module for the exact state of the object.

In order to use mock objects, we will need to install a module that supports object mocking. There are various types of testing tools and modules available out there. Most of them, however, are designed to test the Node.js's client functionality. There are modules such as JsMockito, a JavaScript fork of the famous Mockito framework for Java, and node-inspector, a module that provides a JavaScript debugger that starts implicitly in the Google Chrome browser.

Native support for the Chrome browser is logical, since Node.js is built on top of the Google V8 JavaScript Engine. As we are developing a server-side application, these are not the most convenient tools, as JsMockito is not pluggable as a Node.js module and using a debugger within your browser to debug backed applications just doesn't seem right to me. Anyway, if you are about to dive deeper into Node.js, you should definitely give it a try.

For testing server-side JavaScript modules, I personally prefer the Sinon.JS module. Like all the other modules, it is available in the NPM repository, so execute the following command to install it: `npm install sinon`

Sinon.JS is a very flexible JavaScript testing library providing functionality for mocking, stubbing, and spying on JavaScript objects. It is available at `http://sinonjs.org` and can be used with any JavaScript testing framework. Let's see what we need in order to test our HTTP module. It exports only one method, `handle_request`, which takes the HTTP `request` and `response` objects as arguments. Based on the requested method, the module calls its internal functions to handle different requests. Each request handler writes a different output to the response.

So, in order to test this functionality in an isolated environment such as Nodeunit, we need mock objects, which will then be passed as arguments. To ensure that the module behaves as expected, we will need to have access to the data stored in those objects.

Working with mock objects

Here are the steps that need to be carried out when using mock objects:

1. Call the `require` function with `sinon` as a parameter and export a `test` function from it:

   ```
   var sinon = require('sinon');
   exports.testAPI(test){...}
   ```

2. Define an API description of the method you want to mock as follows:

```
var api = {'methodX' : function () {},
  'methodY' : function() {},
  'methodZ' : function() {}};
```

3. Use `sinon` within the exported function in order to create mock objects out of the `api` description:

```
var mock = sinon.mock(api);
```

4. Set the expectations on the mock objects. Expectations are set on the mocked objects by describing how the mocked method should behave, what arguments it is supposed to take, and what value it is supposed to return. When the mocked method is called with a state different state than what is described, the expectation will fail when verified later:

```
mock.expects('methodX').once().withArgs('xyz')
.returns('abc');
api.methodX('xyz')
```

> The preceding sample expects that `methodX` gets called exactly once with the `xyz` argument, and it will force the method to return `abc`. The Sinon.JS module makes that possible for us.

> The method of the description object is called and not that of the mocked object. The mocked object is used to set the expectations for the mocked method, and later to check whether those expectations have been fulfilled.

5. Use the mocked object in the test environment, and later, call its `verify()` method. This method will check whether the code being tested interacted correctly with mock, that is, how many times the method has been called and whether it has been called with the expected arguments. If any of the expectations is not met, then an error will be thrown, causing the test to fail.

> The exported `test` function of our test module has an argument. That argument provides assert methods that can be used to check test conditions. In our example, we mocked the method to always return `abc` when called with the `'xyz'` arguments.

So, to complete the test, the following assert can be done, and in the end, the mock object needs to be verified:

```
mock.expects('methodX').once().withArgs('xyz')
.returns('abc');
test.equals(api.methodX('xyz'), 'abc');
mock.verify();
```

Try modifying the arguments passed to `methodX` so that they don't match the expectation, and you will see this breaking your test.

Let's put these steps into practice and create the following `test-http-module.js` file in the `test` directory:

```
var sinon = require('sinon');
exports.test_handle_GET_request = function (test) {
  var response = {'writeHead' : function () {}, 'end':    function() {}};
var responseMock = sinon.mock(response);
  responseMock.expects('end').once().withArgs('Get action
  was requested');
  responseMock.expects('writeHead').once().withArgs(200, {
   'Content-Type' : 'text/plain'});
   var request = {};
   var requestMock = sinon.mock(request);
   requestMock.method = 'GET';
   var http_module = require('../modules/http-module');
   http_module.handle_request(requestMock, response);
   responseMock.verify();
   test.done();
};
```

Start the test with Nodeunit's `test-http-module.js` to verify that it passes successfully. Your next step will be to extend the test so that it covers the handling of all the HTTP methods in our HTTP module.

Deploying an application

Node.js has an event-driven, non-blocking I/O model, which makes it perfect for real-time applications that scale well in distributed environments, such as public or private cloud platforms. Each cloud platform offers tools that allow seamless deployment, distribution, and scaling of its hosted applications. In this section, we will look at two publicly available Node.js application cloud providers—Nodejitsu and Microsoft Azure.

But first, let's spend some time on the clustering support, as it is fundamental for understanding why Node.js fits so well in the cloud environment. Node.js comes with clustering support built in its core. Using the cluster module in your applications allows them to start as many workers as necessary to handle the load they will face. Generally, it is recommended to match the number of workers to the number of threads or logical cores your environment has.

The heart of your application is the master process. It is responsible for keeping a registry of active workers and the load of the application, and to create. It also creates more workers when needed and reduces them when the load decreases.

The cloud platform should also ensure that there is zero downtime when deploying new versions of the applications. In such cases, the master process needs to be notified that a newer version should be distributed. It should fork the new worker's new application version and notify the workers currently running with the old version to close their listeners; thus, it stops accepting connections and exits gracefully once they finish. Therefore, all the new incoming requests will be handled by the newly started workers, and after the obsolete workers terminate, all the running workers will be running the latest version.

Microsoft Azure

Microsoft's cloud platform as a service, Azure, also offers hosting of Node.js applications. They have chosen a slightly different approach, and instead of providing a command-line interface to interact with their repositories, they make use of their Git integration; that is, you interact with Azure as you would interact with any other Git repository. If you are not familiar with Git, I strongly recommend that you learn more about this distributed source code version control system.

If you've chosen Azure as your platform, you will find this link very useful: `http://azure.microsoft.com/en-us/develop/nodejs/`

Nodejitsu

Let's take a closer look at some Node.js's **Platform as a Service (PaaS)** offerings. The first PaaS we will look at is Nodejitsu, available at `https://www.nodejitsu.com`.

This allows seamless deployment of Node.js applications on the cloud, with many useful features for development, management, deployment, and monitoring of Node.js applications. To interact with `jitsu`, you need to install its command-line interface, which is available as a Node.js module:

```
npm install -g jitsu
```

After installing `jitsu` and starting it with `jitsu`, you will be given a warm welcome, with a friendly console screen that will introduce you to the basic `jitsu` commands, as shown here:

```
⊗ ⊖ ⊙   Terminal  File  Edit  View  Search  Terminal  Help
valio@G771JW:~/workspace/test$ jitsu
warn:
warn:        Nodejitsu has been acquired by GoDaddy
warn:
warn:        Read more at: https://nodejitsu.com/godaddy
warn:        Or run:      jitsu godaddy
warn:
info:        Welcome to Nodejitsu
info:        jitsu v0.15.0, node v5.5.0
info:        It worked if it ends with Nodejitsu ok
warn:        You are using unstable version of node.js. You may experience problems.
info:        Executing command
help:
help:              _   _   _   _
help:             / / / /  / /
help:          _/ / /_  _/ /_/
help:
help:        Flawless deployment of Node.js apps to the cloud
help:        open-source and fully customizable.
help:        https://github.com/nodejitsu/jitsu
help:
help:        Usage:
help:
help:           jitsu <resource> <action> <param1> <param2> ...
help:
```

In order to interact with `jitsu`, you will need to sign up for it. `jitsu` offers different pricing plans, starting from $20, as well as free trial services.

You can do that either from their website or with `jitsu signup` command. Then, you can start making use of the tools the command-line interface offers.

Self-test questions

To get additional confidence about your newly gained knowledge, go through the next set of statements and state whether they are true or false:

- Node modules can export more than one function to outer components.
- Node modules are extendable.
- Modules always need to explicitly declare their dependencies to other modules.
- When using mocking in a test environment, the mocked method is called on the mocked object.
- Debugging Node.js code is not as straightforward as other pieces of non-JavaScript code.

Summary

In this chapter, you gained your first Node.js experience, starting from a simple *hello world* application and moving on to a more complex sample HTTP server-like application that handles incoming HTTP requests. Being more confident with Node.js, you refactored the application to use a user defined modules and then created unit tests for your using a mocking framework to eliminate dependencies on complex objects in your test environment.

Now that you've understood how to handle and test incoming HTTP requests, in the next chapter, our next step will be to define what a typical Web API looks like and how it can be tested.

3

Building a Typical Web API

Now that you know what RESTful services are and you feel comfortable with Node.js and its modules, it is time to start with your first RESTful web API implementation. It will be an application that provides mobile phone contacts, represented in JSON format. The application will support different queries based on search criteria passed as GET parameters. For the purpose of this chapter, the contacts data will be read from a static JSON file.

Our first draft API will not support creating or updating contacts at this point, as is done in a real-world application; using file storage for data exposed to millions of users is definitely not an option. We will provide insertion, update, and more complex querying mechanisms for the service later in the book, after we have looked at modern NoSQL database solutions.

We will also cover the topic of content negotiation, a mechanism that allows consumers to specify the expected format of the requested data. Then, we will take a brief look at the cross-origin resource sharing specification, which defines open access across domain boundaries. Finally, we will take a look at several ways we will query our restfully exposed data with HTTP requests.

To sum up, in this chapter, you will learn the following:

- How to specify a Web API
- How to implement routes
- How to query your API
- Content negotiation
- What CORS is
- API versioning

After this chapter, you will be able to completely specify a RESTful API and will be almost ready to start implementing real-life Node.js RESTful services.

Specifying the API

The very first thing that has to be defined for any web API is the operations it will expose. According to the REST principles, an operation is exposed by an HTTP method and a URI. The action performed by each operation should not contradict the natural meaning of its HTTP method. The following table specifies the operations of our API in detail:

Method	URI	Description
GET	`/contacts`	Retrieves all available contacts.
GET	`/contacts/:primary-phone-number`	Retrieves a single contact by its primary phone number.
POST	`/contacts/`	Updates a contact, if it exists. Otherwise, it creates a new contact.
PUT	`/contacts/`	Creates a new contact.
DELETE	`/contacts/:primary-phone-number`	Deletes an existing contact.
GET	`/groups`	Retrieves all available groups that have contacts assigned.
GET	`/groups:group-name`	Retrieves a unique list of all the groups assigned to contacts.
DELETE	`/groups/:name`	Deletes a group from all the contacts it is assigned to.

The second step in our definition phase is to choose the appropriate format for our contact application's data. JSON objects are natively supported by JavaScript. They are easy to extend during the evolution of an application and are consumable by almost any platform available. Thus, the JSON format seems to be our logical choice here. Here is the JSON representation of a contact object that will be used throughout this book:

```
{
"firstname": "Joe",
"lastname": "Smith",
"title": "Mr.",
"company": "Dev Inc.",
"jobtitle": "Developer",
"primarycontactnumber": "+359777123456",
"othercontactnumbers": ["+359777456789", "+359777112233"],
"primaryemailaddress": "joe.smith@xyz.com",
"emailaddresses": ["j.smith@xyz.com"],
```

```
    "groups": ["Dev", "Family"]
}
```

So far, our API has defined a set of operations and the data format to be used. The next step is to implement a custom user module that will export methods that will be bound to each operation by the URI it is exposed with.

To begin with, let's create a new Node.js Express project. Executing `express chapter3` from a terminal from your Eclipse's `workspace` folder will generate a new project for you. Windows users will need to install the `express-generator` module before being able to generate a project.

Next, this project has to be imported into the Enide developer studio. So you have to create an Eclipse project for it. Nodeclipse is a Node.js module that does that. Go ahead and install it globally by executing `npm install -g nodeclipse`. Once installed, run `nodeclipse -p` from the directory created by `express.js` and you will get an Eclipse project, that is, a `.project` file, generated. Finally start your Enide developer studio and navigate to **File** | **Import** | **Existing projects into workspace**. Go to your `workspace` directory and select the directory that `express.js` created for your project:

Importing an express.js project in the Eclipse environment

As you can see, Express has done some background work for us and has created a starting point for our application: `app.js`. It has also created the `package.json` file for us. Let's take a look at each of these files, starting with `package.json`:

```json
{
  "name": "chapter3",
  "version": "0.0.0",
  "private": true,
  "scripts": {
    "start": "node ./bin/www"
  },
  "dependencies": {
    "body-parser": "~1.13.2",
    "cookie-parser": "~1.3.5",
    "debug": "~2.2.0",
    "express": "~4.13.1",
    "jade": "~1.11.0",
    "morgan": "~1.6.1",
    "serve-favicon": "~2.3.0"
  }
}
```

As we created a blank Node.js Express project, we initially have dependencies only to the Express framework, some middleware modules such as `logging module-morgan, body-parser, cookie-parser`, and the Jade template language. Jade is a straightforward template language used to produce HTML code inside templates. If you are interested in it, you can find out more about it at `http://www.jade-lang.com`.

 When you introduce new module dependencies, it is up to you to keep the `package.json` file up-to-date in order to maintain an accurate state of the modules your application depends on.

We will come to what middleware modules are a bit later in the chapter.

For now, we will ignore the content of the public and view directories as it is not relevant to our RESTful service. They contain the autogenerated style sheets and templates files that might be helpful, if one decides to develop a web-based consumer of the services at a later stage.

We've already mentioned that the Express project created a starting point for our web application in `app.js`. Let's take a deeper look at it:

```javascript
var express = require('express');
var path = require('path');
var logger = require('morgan');
var bodyParser = require('body-parser');
```

```
var routes = require('./routes/index');
var users = require('./routes/users');

var app = express();

// view engine setup
app.set('views', path.join(__dirname, 'views'));
app.set('view engine', 'jade');

app.use(logger('dev'));
app.use(bodyParser.json());
app.use(bodyParser.urlencoded({ extended: false }));


app.use('/', routes);
app.use('/users', users);

// catch 404 and forward to error handler
app.use(function(req, res, next) {
  var err = new Error('Not Found');
  err.status = 404;
  next(err);
});

// error handlers

// development error handler
// will print stacktrace
if (app.get('env') === 'development') {
  app.use(function(err, req, res, next) {
    res.status(err.status || 500);
    res.render('error', {
      message: err.message,
      error: err
    });
  });
}

// production error handler
// no stacktraces leaked to user
app.use(function(err, req, res, next) {
  res.status(err.status || 500);
  res.render('error', {
    message: err.message,
    error: {}
  });
});
```

```
module.exports = app;
```

Obviously, the Express generator has done a lot for us as it has instantiated the Express framework and has assigned a complete development environment around it. It has done the following:

- Configured the middleware to be used in our application: `body-parser`, the default router, as well as error handler middleware for our development environment
- Injected a logger instance from the morgan middleware
- Configured the Jade template, as it has been selected as the default template for our application
- Configured the default URI that our Express application will be listening to `/` and `/users` and have created dummy handle functions for them

You will have to install all these modules in order to start the generated application successfully.

The only task that the Express generated application has left us is to specify at which port the application should listen for incoming requests. Let's add that with:

```
app.listen(3000);
```

Start the application from the command line with `node app.js` send a `GET` request to `/users` with the RestClientTool Eclipse plugin, and see what happens:

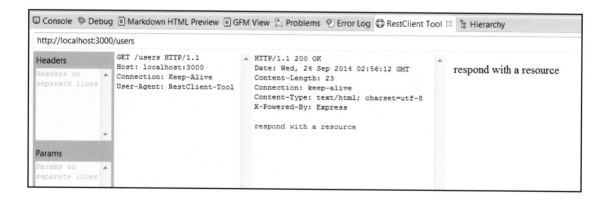

Static response from the automatically generated application

Requesting the /users location has resulted in calling the list function of the user's module, which outputs a static response: respond with a resource.

Our application will not be using a template language and style sheets, so let's get rid of the lines that set the views and view engine properties in the application configuration. In addition, we will be implementing our own routes. Thus, we don't need the bounding of / and /users URIs for our app, neither do we need the user module. So after this cleanup, our application looks a lot cleaner and we are ready to move forward.

Before doing that, though, there is one term that needs to be explained further—middleware functions. It is a subset of chained functions called by the express.js routing layer before the user-defined handler is invoked. Middleware functions have full access to the request and response objects and can modify either of them.

The middleware chain is always called in the exact order in which it has been defined, so it is vital for you to know exactly what a specific piece of middleware is doing. Once a middleware function finishes, it calls the next function in the chain by invoking its next argument as a function. After the complete chain gets executed, the user-defined request handler is called.

Here are the basic rules that apply to the middleware chain:

- A middleware function has the following signature: function (request, response, next).
- Middleware functions are executed in the exact order in which they have been added to the application chain. This means that, if you want your middleware function to be called before a specific route, you need to add it before declaring the route.
- Middleware functions use their third parameter, next, as a function to indicate that they have completed their work and to exit. When the next() parameter of the last function in the chain has been called, the chained execution is completed and the request and the response objects reach the defined handlers.

Now that we know what a middleware function is, let's clarify what the currently used middleware functions provide us with. The body-parser middleware is the Express framework built in a parser. It parses the request body and populates the request object after the middleware execution finishes.

The `express.Router` is the default middleware of `express.js` for routing. It makes our URI mapping work. We will cover routing capabilities in the next section. First, let's move on and implement our user module that will be mapped to our URIs. The module will be named `contacts.js`:

```javascript
var fs = require('fs');

function read_json_file() {
    var file = './data/contacts.json';
    return fs.readFileSync(file);
}

exports.list = function() {
    return JSON.parse(read_json_file());
}

exports.query = function(number) {
    var json_result = JSON.parse(read_json_file());
    var result = json_result.result;

    for (var i = 0; i < result.length; i++) {
        var contact = result[i];
        if (contact.primarycontactnumber == number)      {
            return contact;
        }
    }
    return null;
}

exports.query_by_arg = function(arg, value) {
    var json_result = JSON.parse(read_json_file());
    var result = json_result.result;

    for (var i = 0; i < result.length; i++) {
        var contact = result[i];
        if (contact[arg] == value) {
            return contact;
        }
    }
    return null;
}

exports.list_groups = function() {
    var json_result = JSON.parse(read_json_file());
    var result = json_result.result;

    var resultArray = new Array ();
```

```
        for (var i = 0; i < result.length; i++) {
            var groups = result[i].groups;

            for (var index = 0; index < groups.length; index++) {
                if (resultArray.indexOf(groups[index]) == -1) {
                    resultArray.push(groups[index]);
                }
            }
        }
    }
    return resultArray;
}

exports.get_members = function(group_name) {
    var json_result = JSON.parse(read_json_file());
    var result = json_result.result;
    var resultArray = new Array ();

    for (var i = 0; i < result.length; i++) {
        if (result[i].groups.indexOf(group_name) > -1) {
            resultArray.push(result[i]);
        }
    }
    return resultArray;
}
```

The contacts module is built around the `contacts.json` file, stored in the `data` directory. The content of the source file is read using the File System module, `fs`, within the `read_json_file` function. The File System module provides several filesystem operations such as functions for creating, renaming, or deleting files or directories; truncating; linking; chmod functions; as well as synchronous and asynchronous file access for reading and writing data. In our sample application, we aim to use the most straightforward approach, so we implement a query function that reads the `contacts.json` file by utilizing the `readFileSync` function of the File System module. It returns the content of a file as a string, within a synchronous call. All other functions of the module are exported and can be used to query the content of the source file, based on different criteria.

The contacts module exports the following functions:

- `list`: This returns an array of JSON objects containing all the contacts in the `contact.json` file.
- `query (number)`: This returns a JSON object representing the contact identified uniquely by its primary phone number.

- `query_by_arg(arg, value)`: This returns a JSON object representing the first found contact that is identified by a provided criterion and its value; for example, `query_by_arg('firstname', 'John')` will return the first found contact whose first name is `John`.
- `list_groups()`: This returns a JSON array containing a list of all the groups available in our contacts. The list does not contain duplicates.
- `get_members(group_name)`: This returns an array with JSON objects for all the contacts that are assigned to the group specified by the argument.

Now that we have five complete functions, let's see how to bind them to our Express application.

Implementing routes

In Node.js terms, a route is a binding between a URI and function. The Express framework provides built-in support for routing. An `express` object instance contains functions named after each HTTP verb: `get`, `post`, `put`, and `delete`. They have the following syntax: `function(uri, handler);`. They are used to bind a handler function to a specific HTTP action executed over a URI. The handler function usually takes two arguments: `request` and `response`. Let's see it with a simple `Hello route` application:

```
var express = require('express');
var app = express();

app.get('/hello', function(request, response){
  response.send('Hello route');
});

app.listen(3000);
```

Running this sample at localhost and accessing `http://localhost:3000/hello` will result in calling your handler function and it will respond saying `Hello route`, but routing can give you much more. It allows you to define a URI with parameters; for example, let's use `/hello/:name` as a routing string. It tells the framework that the URI used consists of two parts: a static part (`hello`) and a variable part (the `name` parameter).

Furthermore, when the routing string and the handler function are defined in line with the `get` function of an Express instance, a parameter collection is made available directly in the `request` argument of the handler function. To demonstrate this, let's modify our previous example a bit:

```
var express = require('express');
var app = express();

app.get('/hello/:name', function(request, response){
    response.send('hello ' + request.params.name);
});

app.listen(3000);
```

As you can see in the preceding code snippet, we used a colon (`:`) to separate the parameter part of the URI form the static part. Now requesting `http://localhost:3000/hello/friend` will result in the following output:

```
hello friend
```

This is how we can provide parameterized URIs with Express. It is a nice feature, but it is often not enough. In web applications, we are used to providing additional parameters with `GET` parameters.

Unfortunately, the Express framework is not so good with `GET` parameters. Thus, we have to utilize the `url` module. It is built into Node.js to provide an easy way of using URL parsing. Let's use our `hello` result with other parameters in the application again, but extend it in a way that it outputs `hello all` when `/hello` is requested and `hello friend` when the requested URI is `/hello?name=friend`:

```
var express = require('express');
var url = require('url');
var app = express();

app.get('/hello', function(request, response){
    var get_params = url.parse(request.url, true).query;

    if (Object.keys(get_params).length == 0)
    {
        response.end('Hello all');
    }
    else
    {
```

```
          response.end('Hello ' + get_params.name);
     }
});

  app.listen(3000);
```

There are a few things worth mentioning here. We used the `url` module's function `parse`. It takes a URL as its first argument and a Boolean as an optional second argument, which specifies whether the query string should be parsed or not. The `url.parse` function returns an associative object. We used `Object.keys` with it to transform the keys in these associative objects into an array so that we can check its length. This will help us check whether our URI has been called with GET parameters or not. In addition to the routing functions named after each HTTP verb, there is also a function named `all`. When used, it routes all the HTTP actions to the specified URI.

Now that we know how routing and the GET parameters work within Node.js and the Express environment, we are ready to define routes for our contact module and modify our `app.js` file accordingly:

```
var express = require('express');
var path = require('path');

var logger = require('morgan');
var cookieParser = require('cookie-parser');
var bodyParser = require('body-parser');
var contacts = require('./modules/contacts');
var http = require('http');
var url = require('url');

var app = express();

app.get('/contacts',
     function(request, response){
          var get_params = url.parse(request.url,
          true).query;
          if (Object.keys(get_params).length === 0)
          {
               response.setHeader('content-type',
               'application/json');
               response.end(JSON.stringify
               (contacts.list()));
          }
          else
          {
               response.setHeader('content-type',
```

```
                'application/json');
                response.end(JSON.stringify
                (contacts.query_by_arg(get_params.arg,
                get_params.value)));
            }
        }
);


app.get('/contacts/:number', function(request, response) {
    response.setHeader('content-type','application/json');
    response.end(JSON.stringify
    (contacts.query(request.params.number)));
});

app.get('/groups', function(request, response) {
    console.log ('groups');
    response.setHeader('content-type',
    'application/json');
    response.end(JSON.stringify(contacts.list_groups()));
});

app.get('/groups/:name', function(request, response) {
    console.log ('groups');
    response.setHeader('content-type',
    'application/json');
    response.end(JSON.stringify
    (contacts.get_members(request.params.name)));
});
http.createServer(app).listen(3000, function(){
  console.log('Express server listening on port 3000');
});
```

Each handler function sets the `content-type` header to `application/json`, as we want our service to comply with the REST principles. Thus, it needs to report the MIME type of the data it provides.

Here is a table that nicely describes the routing we just did. We will need this in the next section when we test our API.

HTTP method	Route	Contact's module function
GET	`/contacts`	`list()`
GET	`/contacts/:number`	`query(number)`
GET	`/contacts?arg&value`	`query_by_arg(arg, value)`
GET	`/groups`	`list_groups()`
GET	`/groups/:name`	`get_members(group_name)`

Querying the API

We need some test data in order to test our service, so let's create the `contacts.json` file in the `data` directory of our project:

```json
{
    "result": [{
        "firstname": "Joe",
        "lastname": "Smith",
        "title": "Mr.",
        "company": "Dev Inc.",
        "jobtitle": "Developer",
        "primarycontactnumber": "+359777123456",
        "othercontactnumbers": [
            "+359777456789",
            "+359777112233"
        ],
        "primaryemailaddress": "joe.smith@xyz.com",
        "emailaddresses": [
            "j.smith@xyz.com"
        ],
        "groups": [
            "Dev",
            "Family"
        ]
    },
    {
        "firstname": "John",
        "lastname": "Douglas",
        "title": "Mr.",
        "company": "Dev Inc.",
        "jobtitle": "Developer",
```

```
        "primarycontactnumber": "+359777223344",
        "othercontactnumbers": [],
        "primaryemailaddress": "john.douglas@xyz.com",
        "emailaddresses": [
            "j.douglas@xyz.com"
        ],
        "groups": [
            "Dev"
        ]
    }]
}
```

This data will allow us to test all our five functions. We've already covered the RestClientTool of the Enide Studio. We will continue using it as our primary test tool. Referring to the definition table from the last section, let's perform tests for each operation of our service:

Requesting /contacts should return all the contacts in the test file. In our example, those are Joe Smith and John Douglas. This is shown in the following screenshot:

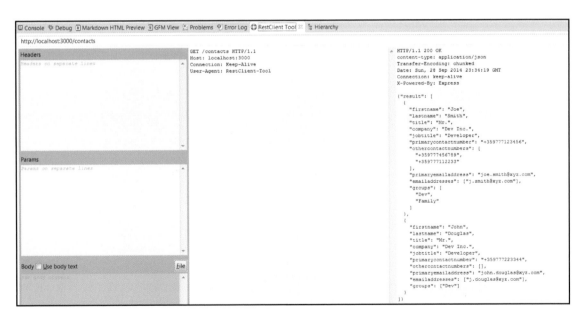

John's primary contact number is +359777223344. Thus, requesting /contacts/%2B359777223344 should result in returning only his contact. Note that the URL encoding/decoding of the + sign is handled implicitly for us by the middleware. Requesting %2B359777123456 will result in returning Joe's contact details as shown next:

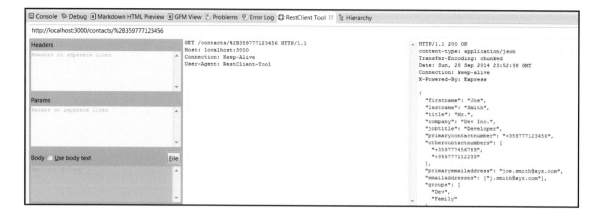

Requesting /contacts?firstname=joe should result in only Joe's contact details being returned.

Requesting /groups will return a list of all groups assigned in our contacts without duplicates, as shown in the next screenshot:

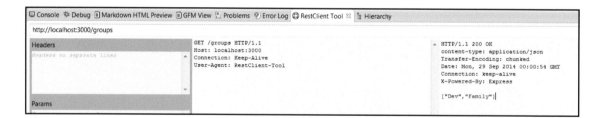

Requesting /groups/Dev will return both Joe and John, as they both have the Dev group assigned. However, /groups/Family will return only Joe.

These five test requests show that the API behaves correctly.

Content negotiation

So far, the contacts service supports only the JSON format, and thus works only with media-type application/json. Let's assume our service has to offer data in different formats, for example, both JSON and XML. Then, the consumer needs to explicitly define the data format they need. The best way to carry out content negotiation in REST has been a very debatable subject for a long time.

In his famous discussion on implementing content negotiation correctly, Roy Fielding states:

> *"All important must have URIs."*

However, that leaves a gap on how to expose the same resource in a different data format, so Roy continues:

> *"Agent-driven negotiation is far more effective, but there was a huge disagreement between myself and the chair of the HTTP working group and my original agent-driven design for HTTP/1.1 was effectively buried in committee. To do negotiation right, the client needs to be aware of all the alternatives and what it should use as a bookmark."*

While one can still choose to stick with a URI-driven negotiation by providing the desired format with custom GET parameters, the REST community has chosen to stick to Roy's suggestion for agent-driven negotiation. Now that it has been almost a decade since this argument was initiated, it has been proven that they took the right decision. Agent-driven negotiation makes use of the Accept HTTP header.

The Accept HTTP header specifies the media type of the resource that the consumer is willing to process. In addition to the Accept header, the consumer may also make use of the Accept-Language and Accept-Encoding headers to specify what language and encoding the results should be provided in. In case the server fails to provide the results in the expected format, it can either return a default value or make use of HTTP 406 Not acceptable in order not to cause data confusion errors on the client side.

The Node.js HTTP response object contains a method, format, that performs content negotiation based on the Accept HTTP header if set in the request object. It uses the built-in request.accepts() to select an appropriate handler for the request. If that is not found, the server invokes the default handler, which responds with HTTP 406 Not acceptable. Let's create a demo on how to use the format method within one of our routes. For that purpose, let's assume we have implemented a function within our contacts module, named list_groups_in_xml, that provides the group data in XML format:

```
app.get('/groups', function(request, response) {
response.format( {
    'text/xml' : function() {
       response.send(contacts.list_groups_in_xml);
    },
    'application/json' : function() {
       JSON.stringify(contacts.list_groups());
    },
    'default' : function() {.
       response.status(406).send('Not Acceptable');
```

```
        }
    });
});
```

This is how you can implement content negotiation in a clear and straightforward way.

Cross-origin resource sharing

Cross-site HTTP requests are HTTP requests for resources loaded from a different domain than what was initially requested. A good example would be an HTTP OPTIONS request that contains headers describing another HTTP request to be made, for example, a GET request for a resource, called actual request. Such requests are usually subject to different security restrictions due to harmful **Cross-Side Scripting** (**XSS**). Over the years, XSS have become famous for allowing injections of different client-side scripts in web-based resources.

Thus, the W3C has recommended the Cross-Origin Resource Sharing mechanism to provide a secure way for web services to support cross-site data transfer. The recommendation is available at http://www.w3.org/TR/cors/. It is built around HTTP request and response headers used to control different aspects of HTTP specification that may be used in XSS to make your application vulnerable to such attacks.

The HTTP request headers are as follows:

- Origin: This defines where the actual request originates from
- Access-Control-Request-Method: This defines the method that should be used for the actual request
- Access-Control-Request-Header: This defines the headers that should be used in the actual request

All valid CORS response headers start with Access-Control-Allow.

The HTTP response headers are as follows:

- Access-Control-Allow-Origin: This is a required header in all valid CORS responses. It either echoes the origin of the actual host that the request has been made from, if that is the only origin allowed to access the resource, or * if it can be accessed from any host.
- Access-Control-Allow-Methods: This is a required header. It lists all the allowed HTTP methods supported by the server providing the resource.

- `Access-Control-Allow-Headers`: This is a required header. If the request contains `Access-Control-Request-Headers`, then it provides a comma-separated list of all the headers accepted by the server providing the resource.
- `Access-Control-Allow-Credentials`: This is an optional header used to indicate that cookies should be included in the CORS request.
- `Access-Control-Expose-Headers`: This is an optional header. Its value is a comma-separated list of headers that should be exposed to the client.
- `Access-Control-Max-Age`: This is an optional header that allows you to cache the response for the value specified by it.

Handling these headers according to the CORS recommendation is a rather difficult task, a bit beyond our current topic of RESTful services. There is a `cors` npm package that we can use to enable `cors` within our Express application. It provides a piece of middleware that enables `cors` within the Express application. Executing `npm install cors` will install the package. We can either enable the `cors` module for the entire application, by passing a piece of `cors` middleware to the `app.use` function, or enable it for one of our routes, for example, in `/contacts/:number`:

```
app.get('/contacts/:number', cors(), function(request, response) {
    response.setHeader('content-type',
    'application/json');
    response.end(JSON.stringify(contacts.query(request.params.number)));
});
```

Handling a GET request to `/contacts/ %2B359777123456` will now result in the `Access-Control-Allow-Origin: *` header becoming a part of the response.

 Refer to the website of the `node-cors` package for more complex examples with `cors` at `http://github.com/troygoode/node-cors`.

API versioning

It is an inevitable fact that all application APIs evolve. However, the evolution of public APIs with an unknown number of consumers, such as RESTful services, is a sensitive topic. As consumers may not be able to handle the modified data appropriately and there is no way of notifying all of them, we need to keep our APIs as backward-compatible as possible. One way to do so is to use different URIs for different versions of our application. Currently, our contacts API is available at `/contacts`.

When the time is right for a new version, for example, Version 2, we need to keep the previous version available at another URI for backward compatibility. I would use `/v1/contacts/or contacts?version=1` and keep `/contacts` mapped to the latest version. Thus, requesting `/contacts` will cause a redirect to `/v2/contacts` or `contacts?version=2` and will make use of the HTTP `3xx` status codes to indicate the redirection to the latest version.

Another option for versioning would be to keep the URI your API stable and rely on custom HTTP headers that will specify the version. But personally, I don't find that a very stable approach concerning backward compatibility as it is much more natural to modify a URL of a request in an application rather than modify the headers that are sent within the request.

Self-test questions

To get additional confidence, go through this set of statements and state whether they are true or false:

- A rest-enabled endpoint must support all HTTP methods relevant to the rest principles
- In the case of a failed content negotiation, it is up to the API to decide whether to return status `406 Not accepted` or the data in a default format, which is different from the requested format
- `Access-Control-Allow-Origin`, `Access-Control-Allow-Methods`, and `Access-Control-Allow-Headers` are all mandatory CORS `response` headers
- When using parameterized routes, the developer can specify the type of the parameter, for example, whether it is a numeric or a literal type

Summary

In this chapter, we dived into some rather complex topics. Let's sum up what we covered. We started by specifying the operations of our Web API and defined that an operation is a combination of a URI and HTTP action. Next, we implemented routes and bound them to an operation. Then we requested each operation using the RestClientTool of the Enide Studio to request the URIs that we routed. In the content negotiation section, we handled the `Accept` HTTP header to provide the results in the format requested by consumers. Then, we had a brief look at the CORS recommendation, and you learned how to enable it via middleware provided by the CORS package. Finally, we covered the topic of API versions that allow us to develop backward-compatible APIs.

We used old-fashioned filesystem storage for our data in this chapter. This is not suitable for a web application. Thus, we will look into modern, scalable, and reliable NoSQL storage in the next chapter.

4
Using NoSQL Databases

So far, we've talked of modern, scalable, and robust RESTful web services. We also implemented an application that exposed a sample service that provides mobile contacts data. However, we introduced a huge bottleneck in this implementation using file storage. It prevents our application from being heavily loaded, as file storage lacks multitenant support. In other words, we definitely need to look for a better storage solution, which can be scalable easily, together with our REST-enabled application. These days, the so-called NoSQL databases are used heavily in cloud environments. They have the following advantages over traditional transactional SQL databases:

- They are **schemaless**, that is, they work with object representations rather than store the object state in one or several tables, depending on their complexity.
- They are **extendable**, because they store an actual object. Data evolution is supported implicitly, so all you need to do is just call the operation that stores the object.
- They are designed to be **highly distributed** and **scalable**.

Nearly all modern NoSQL solutions out there support clustering and can scale further, along with the load of your application. Additionally, most of them have REST-enabled interfaces over HTTP, which eases their usage over a load balancer in high-availability scenarios. Classical database drivers are usually not available for traditional client-side languages, such as JavaScript, because they require native libraries or drivers. However, the idea of NoSQL originated from using document data stores. Thus, most of them support the JSON format, which is native to JavaScript. Last but not least, most NoSQL solutions are open source and are available for free, with all the benefits that open source projects offer: community, examples, and freedom!

In this chapter, we will take a look at two NoSQL solutions: LevelDB and MongoDB. We will see how to design and test our database models, and finally, we will take a brief look at the **content delivery network (CDN)** infrastructures.

At the end of this chapter, we will decide which NoSQL solution to use further in our contacts service application in order to eliminate our current bottleneck—the filesystem.

Key/value store – LevelDB

The first data store we will look at is LevelDB. It is an open-source implementation developed by Google and written in C++. It is supported by a wide range of platforms, including Node.js. LevelDB is a key/value store; both the key and value are represented as binary data, so their content can vary from simple strings to binary representations of serialized objects in any format, such as JSON or XML. As it is a key/value data store, working with it is similar to working with an associative array—a key identifies an object uniquely within the store. Furthermore, the keys are stored as sorted for better performance. But what makes LevelDB perform better than an arbitrary file storage implementation?

Well, it uses a "log-structured merge" topology, which stores all write operations in an in-memory log, transferred (flushed) regularly to a permanent storage called **Sorted String Table (SST)** files. Read operations first attempt to retrieve entries from a cache containing the most commonly returned results. The size of the reading cache and the flush interval of the writing log are configurable parameters, which can be further adjusted in order to be adequate for the application load. The following image shows this topology:

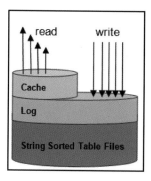

The storage is a collection of string-sorted files with a maximum size of about 2 MB. Each file consists of 4 KB segments that are readable by a single read operation. The table files are not sorted in a straightforward manner, but are organized into levels. The log level is on top, before all other levels. It is always flushed to level 0, which consists of at most four SST files. When filled, one SST file is compacted to a lower level, that is, level 1. The maximum size of level 1 is 10 MB.

When level 1 gets filled, a file goes from level 1 to level 2. LevelDB assumes that the size of each lower level is ten times larger than the size of the previous level. So we have the following level structure:

- Log with a configurable size
- Level 0, consisting of four SST files
- Level 1, with a maximum size of 10 MB
- Level 2, with a maximum size of 100 MB
- Level 3, with a maximum size of 1000 MB
- Level *n*, with a maximum size of the previous level multiplied by 10-*(n-1)*10* MB

The hierarchical structure of this topology assures that newer data stays in the top levels, while older data is somewhere in the lower levels. A read operation always starts searching for a given key in the cache, and if it is not found there, the operation traverses through each level until the entry is found. An entry is considered nonexisting if its key is not found anywhere within all levels.

LevelDB provides `get`, `put`, and `delete` operations to manipulate data records, as well as a batch operation that can be used to perform multiple data manipulations atomically; that is, either all or none of the operations in the batch are executed successfully. LevelDB can optionally use a compression library in order to reduce the size of the stored values. This compression is provided by Google's Snappy compression library. It is highly optimized for fast compression with low performance impact, so too high expectations should not be expected for a large compression ratio.

There are two popular libraries that enable LevelDB usage in Node: LevelDOWN and LevelUP.

Initially, LevelDOWN was acting as foundation binding, implicitly provided with LevelUP, but after version 0.9, it had been extracted out of it and became available as a standalone binding for LevelDB. Currently, LevelUP has no explicit dependency on LevelDOWN defined. It needs to be installed separately, as LevelUP expects it to be available on its Node's `require()` path.

LevelDOWN is a pure C++ interface used to bind Node and LevelDB. Though it is slightly faster than LevelUP, it has some state safety and API considerations, which make it less preferable than LevelUP. To be concrete, LevelDOWN does not keep track of the state of the underlying instance. Thus, it is up to the developers themselves not to open a connection more than once or use a data manipulating operation against a closed database connection, as this will cause errors. LevelUP provides state-safe operations out the box. Thus, it prevents out-of-state operations from being sent to its foundation—LevelDOWN.

Let's move on to installing LevelUP by executing the following npm command:

```
npm install levelup leveldown
```

 Even though the LevelUP module can be installed without LevelDOWN, it will not work at runtime, complaining that it can't find an underlying dependency.

Enough theory! Let's see what the LevelUP API looks like. The following code snippet instantiates LevelDB and inserts a dummy contact record into it. It also exposes a /contacts/:number route so that this very record can be returned as a JSON output if queried appropriately. Let's use it in a new project in the Enide studio, in a file named levelup.js:

```
var express = require('express')
  , http = require('http')
  , path = require('path')
  , bodyParser = require('body-parser')
  , logger = require('morgan')
  , methodOverride = require('method-override')
  , errorHandler = require('errorhandler')
  , levelup = require('levelup');
var app = express();
var url = require('url');
// all environments
app.set('port', process.env.PORT || 3000);
app.set('views', __dirname + '/views');
app.set('view engine', 'jade');
app.use(methodOverride());
app.use(bodyParser.json());
// development only
if ('development' == app.get('env')) {
  app.use(errorHandler());
}

var db = levelup('./contact',  {valueEncoding: 'json'});
db.put('+359777123456', {
  "firstname": "Joe",
  "lastname": "Smith",
  "title": "Mr.",
  "company": "Dev Inc.",
  "jobtitle": "Developer",
  "primarycontactnumber": "+359777123456",
  "othercontactnumbers": [
    "+359777456789",
    "+359777112233"],
```

```
  "primaryemailaddress": "joe.smith@xyz.com",
  "emailaddresses": [
    "j.smith@xyz.com"],
  "groups": ["Dev","Family"]
});

app.get('/contacts/:number', function(request, response) {
  console.log(request.url + ' : querying for ' +
  request.params.number);
  db.get(request.params.number,
function(error, data) {
  if (error) {
    response.writeHead(404, {
      'Content-Type' : 'text/plain'});
    response.end('Not Found');
    return;
    }
  response.setHeader('content-type', 'application/json');
    response.send(data);
  });
});
console.log('Running at port ' + app.get('port'));
http.createServer(app).listen(app.get('port'));
```

As the contact is inserted into LevelDB before the HTTP server is created, the record identified with the +359777123456 key will be available in the database when we execute our first GET request. But before requesting any data, let's take a closer look at the usage of LevelUP. The get() function of LevelDB takes two arguments:

- The first argument is the key to be used in the query.
- The second argument is a handler function used to process the results. It also has two additional arguments:

  Boolean value, specifying whether an error has occurred during the query.

  The actual result entity from the database.

Let's start it with Node's `levelup.js` and execute some test requests with the REST Client tool to `http://localhost:3000/contacts/%2B359777123456`. This can be seen in the following screenshot:

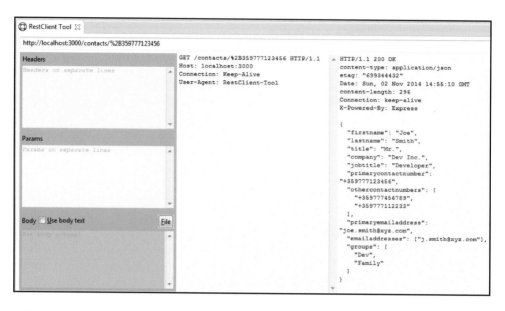

Expectedly, the response is a JSON representation of the contact inserted statically in LevelUP during the initialization of the application. Requesting any other key will result in an "HTTP 404 Not found" response.

This example demonstrates how to bind a LevelUP operation to an HTTP operation and process its results, but currently, it lacks support for inserting, editing, and deleting data. We will improve that with the next sample. It binds the HTTP `GET`, `PUT`, and `DELETE` operations exposed via an Express route, `/contacts/:number`, to the LevelDB's `get`, `put`, and `del` handlers:

```
var express = require('express')
  , http = require('http')
  , path = require('path')
  , bodyParser = require('body-parser')
  , logger = require('morgan')
  , methodOverride = require('method-override')
  , errorHandler = require('errorhandler')
  , levelup = require('levelup');
var app = express();
var url = require('url');
```

```
// all environments
app.set('port', process.env.PORT || 3000);
app.set('views', __dirname + '/views');
app.set('view engine', 'jade');

app.use(methodOverride());
app.use(bodyParser.json());

// development only
if ('development' == app.get('env')) {
  app.use(errorHandler());
}

var db = levelup('./contact',  {valueEncoding: 'json'});

app.get('/contacts/:number', function(request, response) {

  console.log(request.url + ' : querying for ' +
  request.params.number);

  db.get(request.params.number, function(error, data) {
    if (error) {
      response.writeHead(404, {
        'Content-Type' : 'text/plain'});
      response.end('Not Found');
      return;
    }
    response.setHeader('content-type', 'application/json');
    response.send(data);
  });
});

app.post('/contacts/:number', function(request, response) {
console.log('Adding new contact with primary number' +
    request.params.number);
  db.put(request.params.number, request.body, function(error) {
    if (error) {
      response.writeHead(500, {
        'Content-Type' : 'text/plain'});
      response.end('Internal server error');
      return;
    }
    response.send(request.params.number + ' successfully
    inserted');
  });
});

app.del('/contacts/:number', function(request, response) {
```

```
      console.log('Deleting contact with primary number' +
          request.params.number);
      db.del(request.params.number, function(error) {
        if (error) {
          response.writeHead(500, {
            'Content-Type' : 'text/plain'});
          response.end('Internal server error');
          return;
        }
        response.send(request.params.number + ' successfully
        deleted');
      });
    });

  app.get('/contacts', function(request, response) {
      console.log('Listing all contacts');
      var is_first = true;

      response.setHeader('content-type', 'application/json');
      db.createReadStream()
        .on('data', function (data) {
          console.log(data.value);
          if (is_first == true) {
            response.write('[');
          }
          else {
            response.write(',');
          }
          response.write(JSON.stringify(data.value));
          is_first = false;
        })
        .on('error', function (error) {
          console.log('Error while reading', error)
        })
        .on('close', function () { console.log('Closing db
        stream');})
        .on('end', function () {
          console.log('Db stream closed');
          response.end(']');
        })
    });

  console.log('Running at port ' + app.get('port'));
  http.createServer(app).listen(app.get('port'));
```

Perhaps the most interesting part of the preceding sample is the handler of the `/contacts` route. It writes a JSON array of all the contacts available in the database to the output stream of the HTTP response.

LevelUP's `createInputStream` method exposes a data handler for every key/value pair available. As LevelDB is not aware of the format of its values, we have to use the native `JSON.stringify` method to convert each value to a JSON object, based on which we can implement any kind of login. Let's assume we want a function that flushes to the HTTP response only those contacts whose first name is `Joe`. Then we will need to add filtering logic to the data handler:

```
db.createReadStream()
  .on('data', function (data) {
    if (is_first == true) {
      response.write('[');
    } else {
      response.write(',');
    }

    if (data.value.lastname.toString() == 'Smith') {
      var jsonString = JSON.stringify(data.value)
      console.log('Adding Mr. ' + data.value.lastname + '
      to the response');
      response.write(jsonString);
      is_first = false;
    } else{
      console.log('Skipping Mr. ' + data.value.lastname);
    }
  })
  .on('error', function (error) {
    console.log('Error while reading', error)
  })
  .on('close', function () {
    console.log('Closing db stream');
  })
  .on('end', function () {
    console.log('Db stream closed');
    response.end(']');

  })
```

This looks a bit artificial, doesn't it? Well, this is all that LevelDB can possibly offer us, since LevelDB can search only by a single key. This makes it an inappropriate option for data that has to be indexed by several different attributes. This is where document stores come into play.

Document store – MongoDB

Unlike a key/value store, document stores support indexing and searching for data based on different criteria, for example, attributes of a given document. This brings greater flexibility in comparison to key/value stores. Let's imagine we need to find all contacts belonging to the `Dev` group. With a key/value data store, we will need to iterate through all the records and check individually which records belong to the `Dev` group. In document stores, all we need to do is tell the database to give us the documents that contain the `Dev` value in their groups field, and this is achieved with an expression as simple as `{groups: 'Dev'}`, convenient; isn't it?

MongoDB is an open-source document database with built-in support for the JSON format. It provides a full index support, based on any of the available attributes in a document. It is ideal for high-availability scenarios due to its scalability features. MongoDB, available at `https://mms.mongodb.com`, is cloud-ready with its management services, **MongoDB Management Services (MMS)**. They utilize and automate most development operations that need to be carried out to keep your cloud database in good shape, taking care of upgrades, further scaling, backups, recovery, performance, and security alerts.

Let's move forward and install MongoDB. Installers for Windows, Linux, Mac OS X, and Solaris are available at `http://www.mongodb.org/downloads`. Linux users can find MongoDB in all popular distribution repositories, while Windows users can make use of a user-friendly wizard which will guide you through the installation steps where, for a typical installation, all you need to do is accept the license agreement and provide an installation path. And your installation is complete! This is shown in the following screenshot:

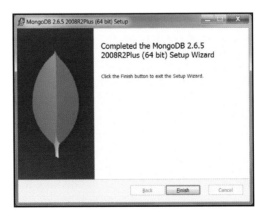

After a successful installation, execute the following command to start MongoDB. If you want to specify a custom data store, you have to use the `--dbpath` argument. Optionally, you can start the MongoDB HTTP console via the `--rest` argument:

```
mongod --dbpath ./data --rest
```

The default port for communicating with MongoDB is `27017`, and its HTTP console is implicitly configured to use a port higher than the data port by a value of 1000. Therefore, the default port of the console will be `28017`. The HTTP console provides useful information about the database such as logs, health status, available databases, and so on. I strongly advise you to spend some time with it. The console can also be used as a RESTful health check service of the database because it provides JSON-encoded information about the running database services and the last error that occurred:

```
GET /replSetGetStatus?text=1 HTTP/1.1
Host: localhost:28017
Connection: Keep-Alive
User-Agent: RestClient-Tool
HTTP/1.0 200 OK
Content-Length: 56
Connection: close
Content-Type: text/plain;charset=utf-8
{
"ok": 0,
"errmsg": "not running with --replSet"
}
```

This REST interface can be used in a script or an application to automate altering notifications providing the current state of the database engine and so on.

The log section of the console shows that your server is running successfully if it is. Then we are ready to move further and see how to connect Node.js to MongoDB.

Database modeling with Mongoose

Mongoose is a modulethat connects Node.js to MongoDB in an **object document mapper (ODM)** style. It offers the **create, read, update, and delete** (also known as **CRUD**) functionalities for documents stored in the database. Mongoose defines the structure of the used documents using schemas. The schema is the smallest unit of data definition in Mongoose. A model is built out of a schema definition. It is a constructor-like function that can be used to create or query documents.

Documents are instances of a model and represent one-to-one mapping to the documents stored in MongoDB. The schema-model-document hierarchy provides a self-descriptive way of defining objects and allows easy data validation.

Let's start with installing Mongoose with npm:

```
npm install mongoose
```

Now that we have the Mongoose module installed, our first step will be to define a schema that will represent a contact:

```
var mongoose = require('mongoose');
var contactSchema = new mongoose.Schema({
  primarycontactnumber: {type: String, index: {unique:
  true}},
  firstname: String,
  lastname: String,
  title: String,
  company: String,
  jobtitle: String,
  othercontactnumbers: [String],
  Heprimaryemailaddress: String,
  emailaddresses: [String],
  groups: [String]
});
```

The preceding code snippet creates a schema definition of our contacts. Defining a schema is straightforward and is quite similar to JSON definition, but instead of providing a value, you have to describe its type and optionally provide additional properties for each key. In the case of the contacts application, we need to use the primary contact number as a unique index in order to avoid having two different contacts with the same primary contact number. Thus, apart from defining its type as String, we also use the index attribute to describe that the value of the primarycontactnumber field must be unique for each individual contact.

Mongoose introduces the term **model**. A model is a constructor-like function compiled out of a schema definition. An instance of a model represents a document that can be saved to or read from the database. Creating a model instance is done by calling the model function of a mongoose instance and passing the schema that the model should use:

```
var Contact = mongoose.model('Contact', contactSchema);
```

Model also exposes functions for querying and data manipulations. Assuming that we have initialized a schema and created a model, storing a new contact to MongoDB is as simple as creating a new `model` instance and invoking its `save` function:

```
var john_douglas = new Contact({
   firstname: "John",
   lastname: "Douglas",
   title: "Mr.",
   company: "Dev Inc.",
   jobtitle: "Developer",
   primarycontactnumber: "+359777223345",
   othercontactnumbers: [],
   primaryemailaddress: "john.douglas@xyz.com",
   emailaddresses: ["j.douglas@xyz.com"],
   groups: ["Dev"]
});
var db = mongoose.connection;
mongoose.connect('mongodb://localhost/contacts');
john_douglas.save(function(error){
   if (error) {
     console.log('Error while saving contact for Mr. John
     Douglas');
     console.log(error);
   }
   else {
     john_douglas.save();
     console.log('Contact for Mr. John Douglas has been
     successfully stored');
   }
});
```

Here is how to use the model in order to query for documents representing male contacts belonging to the `Dev` group:

```
Contact.find({groups: 'Dev', title: 'Mr.'}, function(error,  result) {
   if (error) {
     console.error(error);
   }
   else {
     console.dir(result);
   }
});
```

The model also exposes a `findOne` method, which is a convenient way of finding an object by its unique index and then performing some data manipulation on it, that is, for delete or update operations. The following example deletes a contact:

```
Contact.findOne({primarycontactnumber: '+359777223345' },
function(error, data) {
  if (error) {
    console.log(error);
    return;
  } else {
    if (!data) {
    console.log('not found');
      return;
    } else {
      data.remove(function(error){
        if (!error) { data.remove();}
        else { console.log(error);}
        });
    }
  }
});
```

Testing a Mongoose model with Mocha

Mocha is one of the mostpopular testing frameworks for JavaScript; its main goal is to provide an easy way to test asynchronous JavaScript code. Let's install Mocha globally so that we can make it available to any Node.js application that we may develop in the future:

```
npm install -g mocha
```

We will also need an assert library that can be used together with Mocha. The `Should.js` library module is easy to use and it will be our choice, so let's install it globally too:

```
npm install -g should
```

Now that we have our testing modules installed, we need to specify our `testcase` file path in the `package.json` file, let's modify it by adding a test element pointing to Mocha and the `testcase` file in the script node:

```
{
"name": "chapter4",
"version": "0.0.0",
"private": true,
"scripts": {
"start": "node ./bin/www",
```

```
"test": "mocha test/contact-model-test.js"
  },
"dependencies": {
"body-parser": "~1.13.2",
"cookie-parser": "~1.3.5",
"debug": "~2.2.0",
"express": "~4.13.1",
"jade": "~1.11.0",
"morgan": "~1.6.1",
"serve-favicon": "~2.3.0"
  }
}
```

This will tell the NPM package manager to trigger Mocha when the npm test is executed.

Automation of Mongoose tests must not be affected by the current state of the database. To ensure that the results are predictable at each test run, we need to ensure that the database state is exactly as we would expect it. We will implement a module called `prepare.js` in the `test` directory. It will clear the database before each test run:

```
var mongoose = require('mongoose');
beforeEach(function (done) {
  function clearDatabase() {
    for (var i in mongoose.connection.collections) {
      mongoose.connection.collections[i].remove(function()
      {});
    }
    return done();
  }
  if (mongoose.connection.readyState === 0) {
    mongoose.connect(config.db.test, function (err) {
      if (err) {
        throw err;
      }
      return clearDatabase();
    });
  } else {
    return clearDatabase();
  }
});
afterEach(function (done) {
  mongoose.disconnect();
  return done();
});
```

Next, we will implement a Mocha test, which creates a contact:

```
var mongoose = require('mongoose');
var should = require('should');
var prepare = require('./prepare');

mongoose.connect('mongodb://localhost/contacts-test');


var contactSchema = new mongoose.Schema({
primarycontactnumber: {type: String, index: {unique: true}},
firstname: String,
lastname: String,
title: String,
company: String,
jobtitle: String,
othercontactnumbers: [String],
primaryemailaddress: String,
emailaddresses: [String],
groups: [String]
});

var Contact = mongoose.model('Contact', contactSchema);

describe('Contact: models', function () {


  describe('#create()', function () {
    it('Should create a new Contact', function (done) {

      var contactModel = {
      "firstname":"John",
      "lastname":"Douglas",
      "title":"Mr.",
      "company":"Dev Inc.",
      "jobtitle":"Developer",
      "primarycontactnumber":"+359777223345",
      "primaryemailaddress":"john.douglas@xyz.com",
      "groups":["Dev"],
      "emailaddresses":["j.douglas@xyz.com"],
      "othercontactnumbers":
      ['+359777223346','+359777223347']
       };

      Contact.create(contactModel, function (err,
      createdModel) {
        // Check that no error occurred
        should.not.exist(err);
```

```
        // Assert that the returned contact is as expect

        createdModel.firstname.should.equal('John');
        createdModel.lastname.should.equal('Douglas');
        createdModel.title.should.equal('Mr.');
        createdModel.jobtitle.should.equal('Developer');
        createdModel.primarycontactnumber.should.equal('+359777223345');
    createdModel.primaryemailaddress.should.equal('john.douglas@xyz.com');
        createdModel.groups[0].should.equal('Dev');
        createdModel.emailaddresses[0].should.equal('j.douglas@xyz.com');
        createdModel.othercontactnumbers[0].should.equal('+359777223346');
        createdModel.othercontactnumbers[1].should.equal('+359777223347');
        //Notify mocha that the test has completed
        done();
      });
    });
  });
```

Executing the npm test now results in a call against the MongoDB database creating a contact out of the provided JSON object. After insertion, the assert callback will be executing, ensuring that values passed to by Mongoose are the same as the returned ones from the database.

Creating a user-defined model around a Mongoose model

After seeing how a model works, it is time to create a user-defined module, called **conctactdataservice**, which wraps all CRUD operations for a contact. Since we intend to use that module in a RESTful web application, it seems logical to leave the schema definition and the model creation outside the module and have them provided as arguments of each module function. For now, the module will provide an implementation for each CRUD function, starting with a remove() function. It looks up a contact based on its primary contact number and deletes it from the database, if it exists:

```
exports.remove = function (model, _primarycontactnumber, response) {
console.log('Deleting contact with primary number: '
+ _primarycontactnumber);
model.findOne({primarycontactnumber: _primarycontactnumber},
function(error, data) {
    if (error) {
        console.log(error);
        if (response != null) {
            response.writeHead(500, {'Content-Type' :
```

```
                    'text/plain'});
                    response.end('Internal server error');
                }
            return;
        } else {
            if (!data) {
                console.log('not found');
                if (response != null)
                {
                    response.writeHead(404, {'Content-Type' :
                    'text/plain'});
                    response.end('Not Found');
                }
                return;
            } else {
                data.remove(function(error){
                    if (!error) {
                        data.remove();

                    }
                    else {
                        console.log(error);
                    }
                });

                if (response != null){
                    response.send('Deleted');
                }
                return;
            }
        }
    }
});
}
```

The `update()` function takes the request payload as an argument. A valid update request will contain the new state of a `contact` object, represented in JSON format. First, the primary contact number is parsed out of the JSON object. Then a contact lookup is done. If a contact is found with the provided primary contact number, it gets updated. Otherwise, the `update()` function creates a new contact:

```
exports.update = function (model, requestBody, response) {
var primarynumber = requestBody.primarycontactnumber;
  model.findOne({primarycontactnumber: primarynumber},
    function(error, data) {
  if (error) {
    console.log(error);
    if (response != null) {
```

```
        response.writeHead(500,
          {'Content-Type' : 'text/plain'});
        response.end('Internal server error');
          }
        return;
    } else {
        var contact = toContact(requestBody, model);
        if (!data) {
          console.log('Contact with primary number: '+
          primarynumber + ' does not exist. The contact will
          be created.');
          contact.save(function(error) {
            if (!error)
            contact.save();
          });

          if (response != null) {
            response.writeHead(201,
              {'Content-Type' : 'text/plain'});
            response.end('Created');
          }
          return;
        }
        //poulate the document with the updated values

          data.firstname = contact.firstname;
          data.lastname = contact.lastname;
          data.title = contact.title;
          data.company = contact.company;
          data.jobtitle = contact.jobtitle;
          data.primarycontactnumber =
          contact.primarycontactnumber;
          data.othercontactnumbers =
          contact.othercontactnumbers;
          data.emailaddresses = contact.emailaddresses;
          data.primaryemailaddress =
          contact.primaryemailaddress;
          data.groups = contact.groups;
          // now save
          data.save(function (error) {
          if (!error) {
            console.log('Successfully updated contact with
            primary number: '+ primarynumber);
            data.save();
          } else {
            console.log('error on save');
          }
        });
```

```
      if (response != null) {
        response.send('Updated');
      }
    }
  });
};
```

Creating a contact is very similar to updating it. Both the `create()` and `update()` functions use the `toContact()` function to convert a JSON data structure representing a contact to a `model` instance, that is, a contact document:

```
exports.create = function (model, requestBody, response) {
  var contact = toContact(requestBody, model);
  var primarynumber = requestBody.primarycontactnumber;
  contact.save(function(error) {
    if (!error) {
      contact.save();
    } else {
      console.log('Checking if contact saving failed due
      to already existing primary number:' +
      primarynumber);
      model.findOne({primarycontactnumber: primarynumber},
      function(error, data) {
        if (error) {
          console.log(error);
          if (response != null) {
            response.writeHead(500,
              {'Content-Type' : 'text/plain'});
            response.end('Internal server error');
          }
          return;
        } else {
          var contact = toContact(requestBody, model);
          if (!data) {
            console.log('The contact does not exist. It
            will be created');
            contact.save(function(error) {
              if (!error) {
                contact.save();
              } else {
                console.log(error);
              }
            });

            if (response != null) {
              response.writeHead(201,
                {'Content-Type' : 'text/plain'});
              response.end('Created');
```

```
            }
            return;
        } else {
            console.log('Updating contact with primary
            contact number:' + primarynumber);
            data.firstname = contact.firstname;
            data.lastname = contact.lastname;
            data.title = contact.title;
            data.company = contact.company;
            data.jobtitle = contact.jobtitle;
            data.primarycontactnumber =
            contact.primarycontactnumber;
            data.othercontactnumbers =
            contact.othercontactnumbers;
            data.emailaddresses = contact.emailaddresses;
            data.primaryemailaddress =
            contact.primaryemailaddress;
            data.groups = contact.groups;

            data.save(function (error) {
                if (!error) {
                    data.save();
                    response.end('Updated');
                    console.log('Successfully Updated
                    contact with primary contact number: ' +
                    primarynumber);
                } else {
                    console.log('Error while saving contact
                    with primary contact number:' +
                    primarynumber);
                    console.log(error);
                }
            });
        }
    }
  });
    }
  });
};

function toContact(body, Contact) {
  return new Contact(
  {
    firstname: body.firstname,
    lastname: body.lastname,
    title: body.title,
    company: body.company,
    jobtitle: body.jobtitle,
```

```
        primarycontactnumber: body.primarycontactnumber,
        primaryemailaddress: body.primaryemailaddress,
          emailaddresses: body.emailaddresses,
          groups: body.groups,
          othercontactnumbers: body.othercontactnumbers
        });
    }
```

We will also need to provide a means of querying data, so let's implement a function that queries for a contact by its primary contact number:

```
    exports.findByNumber = function (model, _primarycontactnumber, response) {
      model.findOne({primarycontactnumber:_primarycontactnumber},
    function(error, result) {
        if (error) {
          console.error(error);
          response.writeHead(500,
            {'Content-Type' : 'text/plain'});
          response.end('Internal server error');
          return;
        } else {
          if (!result) {
            if (response != null) {
            response.writeHead(404, {'Content-Type' :
            'text/plain'});
            response.end('Not Found');
          }
          return;
        }
        if (response != null){
          response.setHeader('Content-Type',
          'application/json');
            response.send(result);
          }
          console.log(result);
        }
      });
    }
```

Finally, there's a function that lists all the contacts in the database:

```
    exports.list = function (model, response) {
      model.find({}, function(error, result) {
        if (error) {
          console.error(error);
          return null;
        }
        if (response != null) {
```

```
        response.setHeader('content-type',
        'application/json');
        response.end(JSON.stringify(result));
      }
      return JSON.stringify(result);
    });
}
```

The contact data service module will be the foundation of our contact REST service.

Wiring up a NoSQL database module to Express

Now that we have automated tests for the model and a user-defined module which makes use of it, let's build a sample Express-based application exposing this module via HTTP:

```
var express = require('express')
  , http = require('http')
  , path = require('path')
  , bodyParser = require('body-parser')
  , logger = require('morgan')
  , methodOverride = require('method-override')
  , errorHandler = require('errorhandler')
  , mongoose = require('mongoose')
  , dataservice = require('./modules/contactdataservice');
var app = express();
var url = require('url');

// all environments
app.set('port', process.env.PORT || 3000);
app.set('views', __dirname + '/views');
app.set('view engine', 'jade');

app.use(methodOverride());
app.use(bodyParser.json());

// development only
if ('development' == app.get('env')) {
  app.use(errorHandler());
}

mongoose.connect('mongodb://localhost/contacts');

var contactSchema = new mongoose.Schema({
  primarycontactnumber: {type: String, index: {unique:
```

```
  true}},
  firstname: String,
  lastname: String,
  title: String,
  company: String,
  jobtitle: String,
  othercontactnumbers: [String],
  primaryemailaddress: String,
  emailaddresses: [String],
  groups: [String]
});
var Contact = mongoose.model('Contact', contactSchema);

app.get('/contacts/:number', function(request, response) {
  console.log(request.url + ' : querying for ' +
  request.params.number);
  dataservice.findByNumber(Contact, request.params.number,
  response);
});

app.post('/contacts', function(request, response) {
  dataservice.update(Contact, request.body, response)
});

app.put('/contacts', function(request, response) {
  dataservice.create(Contact, request.body, response)
});

app.del('/contacts/:primarycontactnumber', function(request, response) {
dataservice.remove(Contact,
  request.params.primarycontactnumber, response));
});

app.get('/contacts', function(request, response) {
  console.log('Listing all contacts with ' +
  request.params.key + '=' + request.params.value);
  dataservice.list(Contact, response);
});

console.log('Running at port ' + app.get('port'));
http.createServer(app).listen(app.get('port'));
```

To sum up, we routed each function of the contact data service module to an operation of a RESTful service:

- GET /contacts/:number: This calls dataservice.findByNumber()
- POST /contacts: This calls dataservice.update()
- PUT /contacts: This calls dataservice.create()
- DELETE / contacts/:number: This calls dataservice.remove()
- GET /contacts/: This calls dataservice.list()

As we have our operations exposed, we are ready to perform some serious REST testing. The tool we are going to use is SoapUI. It is available for download from http://www.soapui.org, originally designed for testing classical SOAP-based web services. But then, it followed the REST madness and evolved into a comprehensive tool for testing both SOAP and RESTful services, and is now available for almost any platform out there.

After a straightforward installation, start the tool and create a new REST project from the **File** menu, as follows:

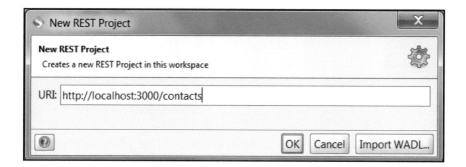

Enter the URI of the contacts service and click on the **OK** button. SoapUI will create a blank test request for you. Create your own requests for each of your module's operations.

Finally, your test project should look similar to what is shown in the following screenshot:

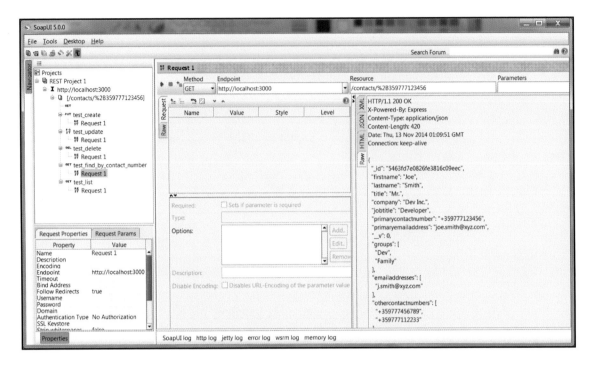

Spend some time in testing each operation together with the test operation in order to gain confidence that the contacts data service module really works.

Content delivery network

RESTful services are now heavily used as feed providers to deliver web content to billions of users globally. Such global services demand a distributed system of data-provisioning servers spread across different data centers globally, assuring high availability and acceptable response times. Global public services, like portals, make use of CDN management software, relying on geographical proximity. This allows content delivery to the nearest or the least loaded available server, resulting in significant performance benefits and few timeouts.

Using a public CDN service to manage your NoSQL contact significantly lowers the **total cost of ownership (TCO)** of your application, allowing it to scale seamlessly, while your application load grows at a minimal price. There are a plenty of CDN offerings available out there. You can choose one of them based on your expected data load, geographical coverage, and many other factors.

MaxCDN (`http://www.maxcdn.com`) is a public CDN service optimized for Node.js and Express. To ease their consumers, they have developed an `express-cdn` module that handles the interaction with the CDN server. More information about the `express-cdn` module is available at `http://www.npmjs.com/package/express-cdn`. A complete example of getting `express-cdn` to work with MaxCDN is available on their blog, at `http://www.maxcdn.com/blog/getting-started-with-maxcdn-s3-and-express`.

Self-test questions

Go through the following questions:

- Describe the difference between a document-oriented database and a key/value data store.
- How would you perform a query with Mongoose for a single value of a multivalued attribute?
- Define a strategy for testing a Node.js module manipulating a NoSQL database.

Summary

In this chapter, we looked at two different NoSQL databases: LevelDB, a key/value datastore, and MongoDB, a much more powerful, document-oriented database. We utilized each of them and utilized Mocha to implement an automated test for the database layer. Now, it is time to decide which database we will use further to build a fully-fledged RESTful web service in the next chapter. The choice is rather logical—because of the document-oriented capabilities, we will proceed with MongoDB.

In the next chapter, we will extend the user-defined module by including support for searching via document attributes, and add filtering and pagination capabilities that will finally evolve into fully-fledged RESTful service implementation.

5

Implementing a Fully-Fledged RESTful Service

In the previous chapter, we exposed our mobile contacts data service via a REST-enabled endpoint for testing purposes. In this chapter, we will use that implementation as a foundation that will evolve into a production-ready service. The first thing to start with is specifying a fixed version of our test implementation; from now on, it will be known as "Version 1". Next, we need to define any new API functionality that will be added in Version 2. This will also include an extension for supporting binary data linked to each contact.

Once deployed on production, the data exposed by our service will grow significantly. Thus, we need to provide it for our consumers in an acceptable way. For that purpose, we will introduce pagination, as well as further filtering capabilities in our API.

Though this contradicts the REST principles, there are cases when caching data responses should be considered as an option. We will look at the benefits and drawbacks of it, and also decide to enable caching when necessary.

Finally, we will dive into the discovery and exploration of REST services.

To sum up, here is what should be further implemented in order to turn the mobile contacts data service into a fully-fledged RESTful service:

- Extensibility and versioning
- Working with arbitrary data
- Linking
- Paging and filtering

- Caching
- Discovery and exploration

Extensibility and versioning

We've already defined a few basic versioning rules in `Chapter 3`, *Building a Typical Web API*. Let's apply them to the test API version implemented in the previous chapter. Our starting point would be to enable the current consumers of the API to continue using the same version on different URIs. This would keep them backward compatible until they test and adopt the new version.

Keeping a REST API stable is not a question of only moving one endpoint from one URI to another. It doesn't make sense to perform redirection and afterwards have an API that behaves differently. Thus, we need to ensure that the behavior of the moved endpoint stays the same, as it has been at the previous location. To ensure that we don't change the previously implemented behavior, let's keep the current behavior from `contactdataservice.js` module to a new module by renaming the file to `contactdataservice_1.js`. Then make a copy of it to a module `contactdataservice_2.js`, where we will introduce all planned new functionality; but before doing that, we have to reroute Version 1 from `/contacts to /v1/contacts/`:

```
app.get('/v1/contacts/:number', function(request, response) {

  console.log(request.url + ' : querying for ' +
  request.params.number);
  _v1.findByNumber(Contact, request.params.number,
  response);
});

app.post('/v1/contacts/', function(request, response) {
  _v1.update(Contact, request.body, response)
});

app.put('/v1/contacts/', function(request, response) {
  _v1.create(Contact, request.body, response)
});

app.delete('/v1/contacts/:primarycontactnumber', function(request,
response) {
    _v1.remove(Contact,
    request.params.primarycontactnumber,
    response);
});
```

```
app.get('/contacts', function(request, response) {
  response.writeHead(301, {'Location' : '/v1/contacts/'});
  response.end('Version 1 is moved to /contacts/: ');
});
```

 We specified the version number at the beginning of the URI—/v1/contacts, because if we had specified it after /contacts as /contacts/v1, we would have corrupted the route for querying a contact by its primary number.

Since Version 2 of our API is not yet implemented, executing a GET request against /contacts will result in the 301 Moved Permanently HTTP status, which will then perform redirection to /v1/contacts/. This will notify our consumers that the API is evolving, and that they will soon need to decide whether to continue using Version 1 by explicitly requesting its new URI, or to prepare for adopting Version 2.

Go ahead and give it a try! Start the modified node application and request /contacts. Then verify that your request is redirected to the newly routed location.

Now that we have finalized Version 1 of the contacts API, it is time to think of further extensions that we can add in Version 2 in order to make it more flexible and functional. Currently, the mobile contacts service supports searching only by the primary contact number. Now it is time to take full advantage of MongoDB, being a document-oriented database, and implement a function that will enable our API consumer to query for contacts based on any of its attributes. For instance, list all contacts for a specific group, or search by first name, last name, or e-mail address. RESTful services usually expose document-oriented data. However, their usage is not limited to documents only. We will extend our contacts service in a way that it also stores binary data—an image that can be linked to a contact. For that purpose, we will use a MongoDB binary format called **Binary JSON (BSON)** in the *Working with arbitrary data* section.

Now, back to the searching extension; we've already used the Mongoose.js model's find() and findOne() functions. So far, we used them to provide the name of the document attribute to be searched with, statically in our JavaScript code. However, this filtering parameter of find() is just a JSON object where the key is the document attribute and the value is the attribute's value to be used in the query. Here is the first new function we will add to Version 2. It queries MongoDB by an arbitrary attribute and its value:

```
exports.query_by_arg = function (model, key, value, response) {
  //build a JSON string with the attribute and the value
  var filterArg = '{"'+key + '":' +'"'+ value + '"}';
  var filter = JSON.parse(filterArg);
  model.find(filter, function(error, result) {
    if (error) {
```

```
      console.error(error);
      response.writeHead(500, {'Content-Type' :
      'text/plain'});
      response.end('Internal server error');
      return;
    } else {
      if (!result) {
        if (response != null) {
          response.writeHead(404, {'Content-Type' :
          'text/plain'});
          response.end('Not Found');
        }
        return;
      }
      if (response != null){
        response.setHeader('Content-Type',
        'application/json');
        response.send(result);
      }
    }
  });
};
```

This function calls find on the model with the provided attribute and value as parameters. We will bind this function to the router's /contacts GET handlers.

In the end, our aim is to have /contacts?firstname=Joe that returns only records for contacts whose first name is Joe, or to have /contacts?groups=Dev return all the contacts in the Dev group. So, we need to extend the handler function of the router a bit.

We will keep the old behavior of returning a list of all available contacts when no parameters are provided within the query string, but we will also parse the query string for the first provided GET parameter in order to pass it and its value to the query_by_arg() function:

```
var _v2 = require(/./modules/contactdataservice_v2');
app.get('/contacts', function(request, response) {
  var get_params = url.parse(request.url, true).query;
  if (Object.keys(get_params).length == 0)
  {
    _v2.list(Contact, response);
  }
  else
  {
    var key = Object.keys(get_params)[0];
    var value = get_params[key];
    JSON.stringify(_v2.query_by_arg(Contact, key, value,
```

```
      response));
    }
  });
```

Perhaps the most interesting part in this function is the URL parsing. As you can see, we keep using the same old strategy to check whether any GET parameters are supplied. We parse the URL in order to get the query string, and then use the built-in Object.keys function to check whether the parsed key/value list contains elements. If it does, we take the first element and extract its value. Both the key and the value are passed to the query_by_arg() function.

You may want to improve Version 2 further by providing support for searching by multiple arguments that are provided by more than one GET parameters. I will leave that to you as an exercise. Now let's test our new function by searching for all contacts in the Dev and Family groups, as shown in the following screenshot:

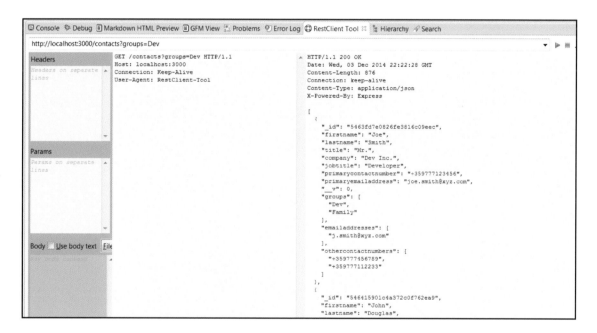

Make sure you spend some more time testing the new functionality with different attributes such as e-mail address, first or last name, and so on.

Working with arbitrary data

MongoDB utilizes BSON as the primary data format. It is a binary format that can store no or many key/value pairs in a single entity called **document**; for example, a sample JSON, `{"hello":"world"}`, becomes `\x16\x00\x00\x00\x02hello\x00\x06\x00\x00\x00world\x00\x00` when encoded in BSON.

The main advantage of BSON over JSON is that it actually stores data, not just literals. For instance, if a long integer number needs to be a part of the document, it will not have to be converted programmatically from a literal to a number. It is also useful when a document needs to have some data bound to it. JSON will usually represent such data as base64-encoded bytes, but that is obviously not the most efficient way.

Mongoose schemas enable storing binary content in the BSON format via the SchemaTypes buffer. It can store binary content (image, ZIP archive, and so on) up to 16 MB. The reason behind the limitation to storage size is rather historical as a means of prevention against excessive usage of memory and bandwidth during transmission.

The GridFS specification was defined in order to address the BSON limitation and to enable working with data larger than 16 MB. GridFS divides data into chunks stored as separate documents. Each chunk, by default, has a size of up to 255 KB. When data is requested from the data store, the GridFS driver retrieves the needed chunks and returns them in an assembled order, as if they had never been divided. Not only does this mechanism allow storage of data larger than 16 MB, but it also enables consumers to retrieve data in portions so that it doesn't have to be loaded completely into the memory. Thus, the specification implicitly enables streaming support.

GridFS actually offers more—it can also store metadata for given data, for example, its format, a filename, size, and so on. This metadata is stored in a separate file and is available for more complex queries. There is a very usable Node.js module called `gridfs-stream`. It enables easy streaming of data in and out of MongoDB, as on all other modules it is installed as an `npm` page. So, let's install it and see how it is used:

```
npm install gridfs-stream
```

To create a `Grid` instance, you are required to have a connection opened to the database:

```
var mongoose = require('mongoose')
  , Grid = require('gridfs-stream');

mongoose.connect('mongodb://localhost/contacts');
var mongodb = mongoose.connection;
var gfs = Grid(mongodb.db, mongoose.mongo);
```

Afterwards, the `createReadStream()` and `createWriteStream()` functions can be conveniently used to read data from and write data to MongoDB. Each piece of data streamed into the database must have its `ObjectId` parameter set. This parameter will identify each piece uniquely, just as it would have identified any other document in MongoDB, and will allow us to delete it from the MongoDB collection by this ID.

Now that the main functions of GridFS are clear, let's extend the contacts service with functions for fetching, adding, and deleting an image assigned to a contact. The service will support only one image per contact, so there will be a single function responsible for adding an image. It will overwrite an existing image each time it is invoked, so an appropriate name for it is `updateImage`:

```
exports.updateImage = function(gfs, request, response) {
  var _primarycontactnumber
  request.params.primarycontactnumber;
  console.log('Updating image for primary contact number:'
  +_primarycontactnumber);
  request.pipe(gfs.createWriteStream({
    _id : _primarycontactnumber,
    filename : 'image',
    mode : 'w'
  }));
  response.send("Successfully uploaded image for primary
  contact number: "+ _primarycontactnumber);
};
```

As you can see, all we need to do in order to flush the data in MongoDB is to create a GridFS write stream. It requires some options that provide the `ObjectId` of the MongoDB entry and some additional metadata such as a title as well as the writing mode. Then we simply call the pipe function of the request. Piping will result in flushing the data from the request to the write stream, and in this way, it will be safely stored in MongoDB:

Retrieving an image is done the other way around: a read stream is created with options, specifying the `_id` of the arbitrary data, optional file name, and read mode:

```
exports.getImage = function(gfs, _primarycontactnumber, response) {
  console.log('Requesting image for primary contact
  number: ' + _primarycontactnumber);
  var imageStream = gfs.createReadStream({
    _id : _primarycontactnumber,
    filename : 'image',
    mode : 'r'
  });

  imageStream.on('error', function(error) {
    response.send('404', 'Not found');
```

```
    return;
  });

  response.setHeader('Content-Type', 'image/jpeg');
  imageStream.pipe(response);
};
```

Before piping the read stream to the response, an appropriate `Content-Type` header has to be set so that the arbitrary data can be rendered in the desired format, `image/jpeg` in our case.

Deleting arbitrary data from MongoDB is not as straightforward. Currently, `gridfs-stream` does not provide that functionality, though the `gridfs-stream` module provides a `remove()` function. This function currently does not behave as expected, and calling it with the appropriate object will not result in deletion. Perhaps, this problem will be addressed in future versions, as `gridfs-stream` is quite young. Currently, the only possible way to delete an arbitrary `gridfs-stream` entry from MongoDB is to remove it from the collection where `mongo.db` stores binary data. This is the `fs.files` collection:

```
exports.deleteImage = function(gfs, mongodb, _primarycontactnumber,
response) {
  console.log('Deleting image for primary contact number:'
  + _primarycontactnumber);
  var collection = mongodb.collection('fs.files');
  collection.remove({_id: _primarycontactnumber,
  filename: 'image'},
  function (error, contact) {
    if (error) {
      console.log(error);
      return;
    }

    if (contact === null) {
      response.send('404', 'Not found');
      return;
    }
    else {
      console.log('Successfully deleted image for primary
      contact number:' + _primarycontactnumber);
    }
  });
  response.send('Successfully deleted image for primary
  contact number: ' + _primarycontactnumber);
}
```

Now, it is time to bind the new functionality to the appropriate routes and give it a try:

```
app.get ('/v2/contacts/:primarycontactnumber/image',
function(request, response){
  var gfs = Grid(mongodb.db, mongoose.mongo);
  _v2.getImage(gfs, request.params.primarycontactnumber,
  response);
})

app.get ('/contacts/:primarycontactnumber/image',
function(request, response){
  var gfs = Grid(mongodb.db, mongoose.mongo);
  _v2.getImage(gfs, request.params.primarycontactnumber,
  response);
})

app.post ('/v2/contacts/:primarycontactnumber/image',
function(request, response){
  var gfs = Grid(mongodb.db, mongoose.mongo);
  _v2.updateImage(gfs, request, response);
})

app.post ('/contacts/:primarycontactnumber/image',
function(request, response){
  var gfs = Grid(mongodb.db, mongoose.mongo);
  _v2.updateImage(gfs, request, response);
})

app.put ('/v2/contacts/:primarycontactnumber/image',
function(request, response){
  var gfs = Grid(mongodb.db, mongoose.mongo);
  _v2.updateImage(gfs, request, response);
})

app.put ('/contacts/:primarycontactnumber/image',
function(request, response){
  var gfs = Grid(mongodb.db, mongoose.mongo);
  _v2.updateImage(gfs, request, response);
})

app.delete('/v2/contacts/:primarycontactnumber/image',
function(request, response){
  var gfs = Grid(mongodb.db, mongoose.mongo);
  _v2.deleteImage(gfs, mongodb.db,
  request.params.primarycontactnumber, response);
})
app.delete('/contacts/:primarycontactnumber/image',
function(request, response){
```

```
    var gfs = Grid(mongodb.db, mongoose.mongo);
    _v2.deleteImage(gfs, mongodb.db,
    request.params.primarycontactnumber, response);
})
```

 Since Version 2, at the time of writing, is the latest version of our API. Any new functionality exposed by it should be available at both locations: /contacts and /v2/contacts.

Let's use the RestClient tool to post an image to /contacts/%2B359777123456.

The following request for a contact's image from a web browser to that URI will display the uploaded image, as shown in this screenshot:

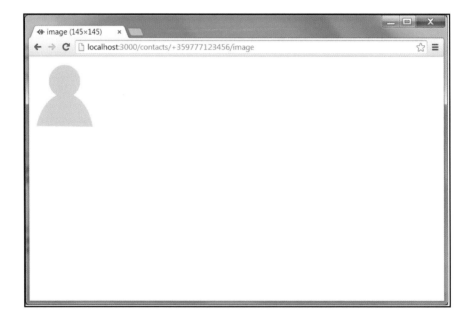

Linking

Now that Version 2 of the contact service supports two data formats: JSON for storing contacts and binary format for storing an image file associated with a contact, we need to ensure that these data formats are not mixed. In the previous section, *Working with arbitrary data*, the information stored for a contact was extended with an additional file entry in MongoDB that stored the binary representation of a JPEG image.

However, none of the JSON models in previously exposed routes, `/v2/contacts` or `/v2/contacts/{primary-number}`, adopted that change, and the image was exposed in a new route:`/v2/contacts/{primary-number|}/image`. That was done intentionally, and keeping backward compatibility was not the main reason for that decision. Mixing literally encoded and binary data in one format is never a good idea. It increases the complexity of the application and makes it error-prone. Thus, we would want to prevent a JSON representation of a contact from looking like this:

```
{
    "firstname": "Joe",
    "lastname": "Smith",
    "title": "Mr.",
    "company": "Dev Inc.",
    "jobtitle": "Developer",
    "primarycontactnumber": "+359777123456",
    "othercontactnumbers": [
        "+359777456789",
        "+359777112233"
    ],
    "primaryemailaddress": "joe.smith@xyz.com",
    "emailaddresses": [
        "j.smith@xyz.com"
    ],
    "groups": [
        "Dev",
        "Family"
    ],
    "image":"
```
iVBORw0KGgoAAAANSUhEUgAAAJEAAACRCAMAAAD0BqoRAAAAGXRFWHRTb2Z0d2FyZQBBZG9iZSB
JbWFnZVJlYWR5ccllPAAAAyJpVFh0WE1MOmNvbS5hZG9iZS54bXAAAAAAADw/eHBhY2tldCBiZW
dpbj0i77u/IiBpZD0iVzVNME1wQ2VhaUh6cmVUek5UY3prYZlkIj8+IDx4OnhtcG1ldGEgeG1sb
nM6eD0iYWRvYmU6bnM6bWV0YS8iIHg6eG1wdGs9IkFkb2JlIFhNUCBDb3JlIDUuMC1jMDYwIDYx
LjEzNDc3NywgMjAxMC8wMi8xMi0xNzozMjowMCAgICAgICAgIj4gPHJkZjpSREYgeG1sbnM6cmR
mPSJodHRwOi8vd3d3LnczLm9yZy8xOTk5LzAyLzIyLXJkZi1zeW50YXgtbnMjIj4gPHJkZjpEZX
NjcmlwdGlvbiByZGY6YWJvdXQ9IiIgeG1sbnM6eG1wPSJodHRwOi8vbnMuYWRvYmUuY29tL3hhc
C8xLjAvIiB4bWxuczp4bXBNTT0iaHR0cDovL25zLmFkb2JlLmNvbS94YXAvMS4wL21tLyIgeG1s
bnM6c3RSZWY9Imh0dHA6Ly9ucy5hZG9iZS5jb20veGFwLzEuMC9zVHlwZS9SZXNvdXJjZVJlZiM
iIHhtcDpDcmVhdG9yVG9vbD0iQWRvYmUgUGhvdG9zaG9wIENTNSBNYWNpbnRvc2giIHhtcE1NOk
luc3RhbmNlSUQ9InhtcC5paWQ6MjMwNjQ1NDdFNjJCNTFFRkI5QzZU4OTFFCMjJCQzEzM0EiIHhtc
E1NOkRvY3VtZW50SUQ9InhtcC5kaWQ6MjMwNjQ1NDhFNjJCNTFFRkI5QzU4OTFFCMjJCQzEzM0Ei
PiA8eG1wTU06RGVyaXZlZZyb20gc3RSZWY6aW5zdGFuY2VJRD0ieG1wLmlpZDoyMzA2NDU0NUU
2MkIxMURGQGQjlDNTg5MUIyMkJDMTMzQSIgc3RSZWY6ZG9jdW1lbnRJRD0ieG1wLmRpZDoyMzA2ND
U0NkU2MkIxMURGQGQjlDNTg5MUIyMkJDMTMzQSIvPiA8L3JkZjpEZXNjcmlwdGlvbj4gPC9yZGY6U
kRGPiA8L3g6eG1wbWV0YT4gPD94cGFja2V0IGVuZD0iciI/Pq3zqsAAAACHUExURdXV1dfX19jY
2NTU1NnZ2dzc3Nra2t3d3f7+/vz8/PHx8eLi4v39/d7e3vn5+fv7+/j4+Pf39+rq6unp6evr6/b
29tvb2+Hh4d/f3/Dw8PLy8vPz8+Pj4+Tk5ODg4fn5/X19e7u7ubm5ujo6OX15e/v7/r6+vvT09O
zs703t7dPT09bW1v///yMJI5sAAASrSURBVHja7NzZUus4EAbglizvu2PHcezsC4T2+z//2AU1w

```
wkJsVbOUPmLOy74kISW7hTQ/22Bp+gpeoqeoqfoKXqKnqL/vcjL2uC0OwVt5v0FouR0tBmj72HM
Pp6SnxQlZUwpwc8hlMZl8kOiKmQUb4WysPoBURVejc6fIyVuEhSlG4aA9wPINqlJUeDi47iBOdG
M4ZSwmSGRvyI4LWTlmxClIeDUQJjqF6UdcIigS3WLohUHaCStIs2iPfKAxm1gr1dUEuQNKXWK2j
lwi2De6hP5NT9oINW+NlFBUCSk0CXKXRASgZtrEu1RNHs9okxwiMZByrSIDiiegw6RH4MwCGJfg
yhwJEROoEG0Qpms1Iv8BUiAYOErF23nUqL5VrnolUrNGn1VLjqiXI7KRbUlBbJq1SIvBikRxJ5i
UepKitxUsSiRFiWKRbktKbLz3y+SnrX8168jP5bcjybfRybvRwtJ0UL1ftSHkrMWKj9FZkTq7Cc
z5aLGkRI5jXLR2ZZZSJZ9Vn+rlTr8px/9HKKCStz8aaFBlEmcI2BnGkR9KDFrYa9DJP5g43mu8Y
iitbBoHWkR9Q0TrNawptcjijpBURdpEvWVI7InWQ5XH4mvMloIHG7AV/TjFPkd8JIAOl+jaLjc8
s6bxVWEFKj5t5xLyXLaXq+oDxgPyWLcbT/+bhbP1s21WYt3/JZXNyUYVzu8t2WGr09r37KXRnqQ
/cvi46fCHdH7twEWL70ZUZ9tiDVC4O5f/Chjh6w3Jer7nYsA37fXsRZrr4uJqkv8uD9j709nQ6J
tYVsTtgB4w7ox0Dnus3KS58PULT3NIi9YWBxbJLyRWaZVlM/IG+e5BuvW0yaKgtjivyFZtEg0iZ
ID7wB9kKxwq0WUh5bos9ZylhpEW5malsXUVyK2UpUItMjOUysKHLkaG1r4GqkUnagkaDzpykidK
JAHjaRCmahlCkDjO6lRJKocQCUB9qJElLmKQGNzNFcgOq+VgcYO8llaFB1BoQjhGMmKdkQlaFjd
O0mRslX931JKpETpQjForElGEiJvg8pFQC4SoiVRP0TD0zsTFqW2BtCQ2hMVHYgWENBAUFQxPUO
E4PpCIq9GTYHvPkf6jaihoIuETiog8m3UF7IREBVUowhowi3y56gzZM8tmlGtInB8TpHvoN7cbW
7D3Wa6ZhHOfS5RqnuIEO+1buFeS0a7COcRhyiy9YOQNhyihhoQ3Wkn3xR5awOTNrzeksmiipkYI
iSHyaKOGBGh7U0URY4ZENLlRNGOGRKR1UTR2tCkDdekaJIoMTVEiLeqk2D81P9j2ropIs9Gc3G8
CaKcGRSx5QSRwUm7ed/+KorRZL5ukl9EGTMqYtlDUUmNimj5UBQSoyISPhJ5ZidtmDbvgWhpXFQ
9EG2IYdGXhQQ/+rd/ayFdiXzTkzY8Sb4XtdS46Pq2fSUqiXHRdQnwWlSvF4s4jl3Xtu353HGcf/
+ZyKcQwUwqAEzu03peFEW+n6bp+ZwkSZZleV5V2+325aVtl0OCIGia02m3210ul9fXsiyKYjabH
Q6bzX6/Px5Xq1XXhWFY1+v151/b3ij5tI/GPEVP0e8U/SPAABPLjHnaJ6XvAAAAAElFTkSuQmCC
"}
```

Imagine how large a result for a non-filtered query could become just for a few hundred contacts if all of them had an image assigned. That is the reason the `toContact()` function did not adopt the newly introduced image field. It was nicely routed to the `/contacts/{primary-number}/image` URI, which uses the `image/jpeg` content type.

With this routing, we also assured linking between an image and a contact, as they share a common unique identifier—the primary contact number of a contact. In this way, a consumer of the service can easily switch from viewing a contact's details to the image by an additional `GET` request to the current contact URI and `/image`. So, we can say that an image is linked to a contact with the `/image` URI.

Implementing paging and filtering

Once deployed to the web, each service becomes available to an enormous number of consumers. They will not only use it to get data but also to insert new data. At some point of time, this will inevitably lead to a large amount of data being available in the database. In order to keep the service user-friendly and maintain a reasonable response time, we need to take care of providing big data in reasonable portions, assuring that it does not need to return a few hundred thousand contacts when the `/contacts` URI is requested.

Web data consumers are used to having various pagination and filtering capabilities. Earlier in this chapter, we implemented the `query_by_arg()` function, which enabled filtering by any of the attributes in our contacts. Now it's time to bring in pagination capabilities, to enable navigation within the result set with the help of a URI parameters.

The `mongoose.js` models can make use of different plugin modules to provide additional functionality on top of them. Such a plugin module is `mongoose-paginate`. The Express framework also provides a piece of pagination middleware named `express-paginate`. It provides out-of-the-box linking and navigation with Mongoose's result pages:

1. Before starting to develop the pagination mechanism, we should install these two useful modules:

   ```
   npm install express-paginate
   npm install mongoose-paginate
   ```

2. The next step will to be to create instances of the `mongoose-paginate` plugin and the `express-paginate` middleware in our application:

   ```
   var mongoosePaginate = require('mongoose-
   paginate'),
   expressPaginate = require('express-paginate');
   ```

3. Initialize the pagination middleware in the application by calling its `middleware()` function. Its parameters specify a default limit and maximum limit of results per page:

   ```
   app.use(expressPaginate.middleware(limit, maxLimit);
   ```

4. Then, provide the `mongoose-pagination` plugin to the `Contact` schema before creating a model:

   ```
   contactSchema.plugin(mongoosePaginate);
   var Contact = mongoose.model('Contact',
   contactSchema);
   ```

5. Finally, call the `paginate()` function of the model to fetch the requested entries in a paginated manner:

   ```
   Contact.paginate({}, {page: requestedPageNumber,
   limit:  requestedPageSize},
   function(error, pageCount, paginatedResults,
   itemCount)  {});
   ```

The first parameter is the filter that Mongoose should use for its query. The second parameter specifies which page is requested, and the third provides the number of entries per page. The results of the paginated query are available in a handler function. Its parameters give us the following information:

- `error`: This specifies whether the query was executed successfully
- `pageCount`: This specifies the number of available pages according to the number of entries per page specified by the third parameter of the model's paginate function
- `paginatedResults`: This is the result entry returned by the query
- `itemCount` : This specifies the number of entries on the current page

The `express-paginate` middleware enables seamless integration of the `mongoose-paginate` module in the web environment by enriching the `request` and `response` objects of an Express handler function.

The `request` objects get two new attributes: `query.limit`, which tells the middleware the number of entries on the page, and `query.page` , which specifies the requested page. Note that the middleware will ignore values of `query.limit` that are larger than the `maxLimit` value specified at the middleware's initialization. This prevents the consumer from overriding the maximum limit and gives you total control over your application.

The RESTful services implementing usable paging need to return the total number of available pages to their consumer. The current result set of the contact service, consisting of a list of JSON objects, lacks such information and needs to be enriched. We will implement this by extending the returned JSON with additional metadata attributes:

```
{
  "object": "contacts",
  "page_count": 2,
  "result": [
    {
      "_id": "5463fd7e0826fe3816c09eec",
      "firstname": "Joe",
      "lastname": "Smith",
      "title": "Mr.",
      "company": "Dev Inc.",
      "jobtitle": "Developer",
      "primarycontactnumber": "+359777123456",
      "primaryemailaddress": "joe.smith@xyz.com",
      "__v": 0,
      "image": "",
      "groups": [
        "Dev",
```

```
      "Family"
    ],
    "emailaddresses": [
      "j.smith@xyz.com"
    ],
    "othercontactnumbers": [
      "+359777456789",
      "+359777112233"
    ]
  }
 ]
}
```

The `object` attribute is just a title to indicate what kind of information is stored in the result set. The `page_count` attribute provides the total number of pages, and the returned contacts are stored as the value of the `result` attribute. Yes, we just partially lost our backward compatibility against Version 1, but it is still available at the `/v1/contacts` URI.

Let's implement a function named `paginate` in the `contactdataservice_v2.js` module. We will delegate the calling of the `paginate` function of the contact model to it:

1. The limit and the request page number are obtained directly from the `request` object, thanks to the `express-paginate` middleware integration:

```
exports.paginate = function (model, request,
response) {

  model.paginate({},
{page:request.query.page,limit:request.query.limit},
    function(error, pageCount, result, itemCount) {
      if (error) {
        console.error(error);
        response.writeHead(500, {
          'Content-Type' : 'text/plain'});
        response.end('Internal server error');
        return;
      }

      response.json({
        object: 'contacts',
        page_count: pageCount,
          result: result
      });

    });
  }
```

2. The final step to enable pagination is to modify the `/v2/contact` route to start making use of the newly created function:

```
app.get('/v2/contacts', function(request, response) {
  var get_params = url.parse(request.url,
  true).query;

  if (Object.keys(get_params).length == 0)
  {
    _v2.paginate(Contact, request, response);
  }
  else
  {
    if (get_params['limit'] != null ||
    get_params['page']!=null)
      {
        _v2.paginate(Contact, request, response);
      }
      else
      {
        var key = Object.keys(get_params)[0];
        var value = get_params[key];
        _v2.query_by_arg(Contact, key, value,
        response);
      }
  }
});
```

3. We will use HTTP status `302 Found` for the default route, `/contacts`. In this way, all incoming requests will be redirected to `/v2/contacts`:

```
app.get('/contacts', function(request, response) {
  var get_params = url.parse(request.url,
  true).query;
  console.log('redirecting to /v2/contacts');
  response.writeHead(302, {'Location' :
  '/v2/contacts/'});
  response.end('Version 2 is found at URI
  /v2/contacts/ ');
});
```

Using an appropriate status code for redirection here is vital to the life cycle of any RESTful web service. Returning `302 Found`, followed by a redirection, ensures that the consumer of the API will always have its latest version available at that location. Furthermore, it is also good practice from the development point of view to use redirection instead of code duplication here.

When you are between two versions, you should always consider using the HTTP 301 Moved Permanently status to show where the previous version has been moved and the HTTP 302 Found status to show the actual URI of the current version.

Now, back to pagination; as the requested page and the limit number are provided as GET parameters and we don't want to mix that up with the filtering capabilities, there is an explicit check for them. Pagination will be used only when either the page or limit GET parameters are available in the request. Otherwise, searching will be carried out.

Initially, we set the maximum limit of 100 results and a default limit of 10, so before trying the new pagination functionality, make sure you insert more contacts than the default limit in the database. This will make the test results more obvious.

Now, let's give it a try. Requesting /contacts?limit=2 will result in returning a list containing only two contacts, as shown in the following screenshot:

As you can see in the example, the total number of pages is 20. This shows that there are exactly 40 contacts stored in the database. Since we didn't specify a `page` parameter in the request, the pagination implicitly returned the first page. To navigate to the next page, simply add `&page=2` to the URI.

Also try changing the `limit` attribute, requesting `/contacts?limit=4`. This will return the first four contacts, and the response will show that the total number of pages is five. Requesting just `/contacts` will make use of the default page limit, which is `10`. Thus, the result will report that there are only two pages to navigate within.

Caching

When we discussed the REST principles defined by Roy Fielding, we mentioned that caching was a rather sensitive topic. In the end, our consumers would expect up-to-date results when executing a query. However, from a statistical point of view, data exposed in the web is more likely to be read rather than updated or deleted.

So it is reasonable that some resources exposed by a public URL become a subject of millions of requests, considering taking off part of the load from the server to a cache. The HTTP protocol allows us to cache some responses for a given period of time. For instance, when multiple requests are received in a short period of time, querying for contacts of a given group, such as `/contacts?groups=Dev`, our service could utilize special HTTP headers that would force the HTTP server to cache the response for a defined time period. This would prevent redundant requests to the underlying database server.

Caching at the HTTP server level is achieved via special response headers. The HTTP server uses a `Cache-Control` header to specify how long a given response should be cached. The period before the cache needs invalidation is set via its `max-age` attribute, and its value is provided in seconds. Of course, there is a nice Node.js module that provides a middleware function for caching, called `express-cache-control`.

Supplying the Cache-Control header in Express applications

Let's install it with the NPM package manager:

```
npm install  express-cache-control
```

Enabling caching with the `express-cache-control` middleware requires three straightforward steps:

1. Get the module:

   ```
   CacheControl = require("express-cache-control")
   ```

2. Create an instance of the middleware:

   ```
   var cache = new CacheControl().middleware;
   ```

3. Bind the middleware instance to the routes you want to enable caching for:

   ```
   app.get('/contacts', cache('minutes',1),
   function(request,
   response) {
     var get_params = url.parse(request.url,
     true).query;

     if (Object.keys(get_params).length == 0)
     {
       _v1.list(Contact, response);
     }
     else
     {
       var key = Object.keys(get_params)[0];
       var value = get_params[key];

       JSON.stringify(_v2.query_by_arg(Contact, key,
       value, response));
     }
   })
   ```

Usually, common URIs that provide many result entries should be the subject of caching, rather than URIs providing data for a concrete entry. In our application, only the `/contacts` URI will make use of caching. The `max-age` attribute must be selected according to the load of your application in order to minimize inaccurate responses.

Let's test our changes by requesting /contacts with the RestClient tool:

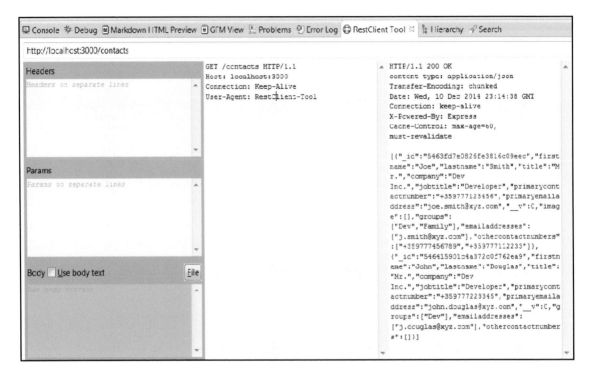

As expected, the express-cache-control middleware has done its job—the Cache-Control header is now included in the response. The must-revalidate option ensures that the cache content is invalidated after the max-age interval expires. Now, if you make another request for a specific contact, you will see that the response does not make use of the express-cache-control middleware, which is because it needs to be explicitly provided in each individual route. It will not be used in URIs deriving from one another.

Responses from GET requests against /v1/contacts, /contacts?firstname=Joe, or /contacts?firstname=Joe will not contain the Cache-Control header, as it is supported only in Version 2 of our API, and the Cache-Control middleware is used only in the main contacts routes: /v2/contacts or /contacts.

Discovering and exploring RESTful services

The topic of discovering RESTful services has a long and complicated history. The HTTP specification states that a resource should be self-descriptive and that it should be identified uniquely by a URI. Dependent resources should be linked by the dependency using their own unique URIs. Discovering a RESTful service means navigating from one service to another, following the links it provides.

After the invasion of classical SOAP web services, the community got used to having a service described in a separate XML-based resource, named **Web Services Description Language** (**WSDL**). It describes the interface of the service, as well as other metadata such as security policy and endpoint location URI. Classical SOAP web services could make use of **UDDI** (short for **Universal Description, Discovery, and Integration**) repositories, allowing consumers to look for different services and their WSDL files.

There are also other specifications, such as **WS Inspection Language** (**WSIL**), which aggregates a group service's WSDL files. WSIL acts like a service providing metadata for classical SOAP web services. This is needed, as SOAP web services require the WSDL information to generate a client request, and optionally the endpoint URI from that WSDL. RESTful clients, however, are not generated out of any metadata. Thus, they don't require such information. That is why a description file is not mandatory.

In the year 2009, a specification called **Web Application Discovery Language** (**WADL**) was invented. It aims to document every URI exposed from a web application, together with the HTTP methods it supports and the parameter it expects. The response media type of the URI is also described. This is very useful for documenting purposes and is all that a WADL file can provide us in terms of RESTful service provisioning.

Unfortunately, there is currently no Node.js module that can automatically generate a WADL file for a given express route. We will have to manually create a WADL file in order to demonstrate how it is used by other clients for discovery.

The following listing shows a sample WADL file describing the resources available at `/contacts`, `/contacts/{primarycontactnumber}` and `/contacts/{primarycontactnumber}`:

```
<application xmlns="http://wadl.dev.java.net/2009/02"
  xmlns:xsd="http://www.w3.org/2001/XMLSchema"
  xmlns:hy="http://www.herongyang.com/Service">

<doc xml:lang="en" />
<resources base="http://localhost:3000/contacts">
<resource path="/">
<method name="GET">
```

```xml
<request>
<param name="page" type="xsd:int" style="query"/>
<param name="limit" type="xsd:int" style="query"/>
<param name="firstname" type="xsd:string"
style="query"/>
<param name="lastname" type="xsd:string"
style="query"/>
</request>
<response status="200">
<representation mediaType="application/json" />
</response>
<response status="404">
<representation mediaType="text/html" />
</response>
<response status="500">
<representation mediaType="text/html" />
</response>
</method>
</resource>
<resource path="/{primarycontactnumber}">
<method name="GET">
<request/>
<response status="200">
<representation mediaType="application/json" />
</response>
<response status="404">
<representation mediaType="text/html" />
</response>
<response status="500">
<representation mediaType="text/html" />
</response>
</method>
<method name="POST">
<request/>
<response status="200">
<representation mediaType="application/json" />
</response>
<response status="404">
<representation mediaType="text/html" />
</response>
<response status="500">
<representation mediaType="text/html" />
</response>
</method>
<method name="PUT">
<request/>
<response status="200">
<representation mediaType="application/json" />
```

```
</response>
<response status="404">
<representation mediaType="text/html" />
</response>
<response status="500">
<representation mediaType="text/html" />
</response>
</method>
<method name="DELETE">
<request/>
<response status="200">
<representation mediaType="application/json" />
</response>
<response status="404">
<representation mediaType="text/html" />
</response>
<response status="500">
<representation mediaType="text/html" />
</response>
</method>
</resource>
<resource path="/{primarycontactnumber}/image">
<method name="GET">
<request />
<response status="200">
<representation mediaType="image/jpeg" />
</response>
<response status="404">
<representation mediaType="text/html" />
</response>
<response status="500">
<representation mediaType="text/html" />
</response>
</method>
<method name="POST">
<request/>
<response status="200">
<representation mediaType="application/json" />
</response>
<response status="404">
<representation mediaType="text/html" />
</response>
<response status="500">
<representation mediaType="text/html" />
</response>
</method>
<method name="PUT">
<request/>
```

```
<response status="200">
<representation mediaType="application/json" />
</response>
<response status="404">
<representation mediaType="text/html" />
</response>
<response status="500">
<representation mediaType="text/html" />
</response>
</method>
<method name="DELETE">
<request/>
<response status="200">
<representation mediaType="application/json" />
</response>
<response status="404">
<representation mediaType="text/html" />
</response>
<response status="500">
<representation mediaType="text/html" />
</response>
</method>
</resource>
</resources>
</application>
```

As you can see, the WADL format is very straightforward. It basically describes the URI of each resource, providing information about the media types it uses and the status codes that are expected at that URI. Many third-party RESTful clients understand the WADL language and get generate request messages out of a given WADL file.

Let's import the WADL file to a SoapUI project and see what we can do with it. The first step is to create a new REST project:

1. Instead of providing the URI of a REST-enabled endpoint, click on the **Import WADL** button. Another window will pop up, asking you to provide a WADL file.

2. Select the `contacts.wadl` file and import it:

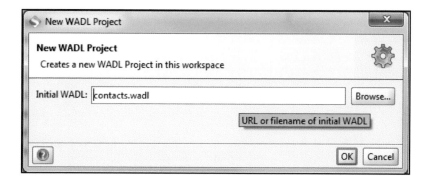

3. After a successful import of the WADL document, SoapUI will have generated a project structure looking like what is shown in the following screenshot:

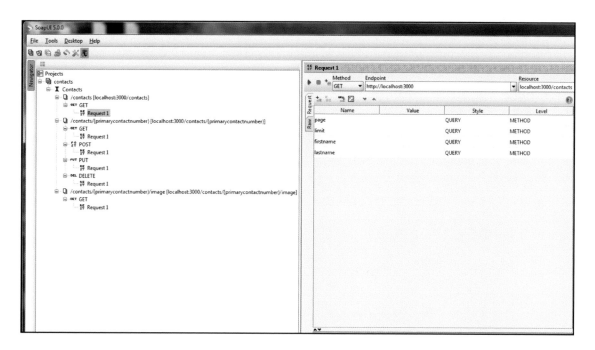

As you can see, the result of importing the WADL file is that we have a project ready to test each aspect of a REST service in the nick of time. This dramatically eases the testing of a REST service.

Self-test questions

Go through the following questions:

- How should a service specify that a resource has been moved permanently to a new location?
- What is the difference between HTTP status codes `301 Moved Permanently` and `302 Found`?
- What is WADL?

Summary

Congratulations! In this chapter, you succeeded in transforming a sample REST-enabled endpoint into a fully-fledged RESTful web service that supports usability filtering and paging. The service delivers both arbitrary and JSON data, and it is ready for high-load scenarios, as it enables caching in its critical parts. One thing that should draw your attention is the appropriate usage of the HTTP status codes when it comes to redirection between new and obsolete versions of any public API.

Implementing appropriate HTTP status is really important for the REST application, so we made use of rather exotic statuses such as `301 Moved Permanently` and `302 Found`. In the next chapter, we will introduce the concept of authorization into our application.

6
Keeping the Bad Guys Out

Once deployed in production, an application is exposed to a large number of requests. Inevitably, some of them will be malicious. This implicitly brings the requirement of granting explicit access permissions. That is, authenticating a selected number of consumers to have access to your service. Most of the consumers will use the service only for data provisioning. However, a few will need to be able to provide new, or modify the existing, contacts data. In order to ensure that only appropriate consumers will be able to execute POST, PUT, and DELETE requests, we will have to introduce the concept of authorization into our application, which will grant only explicitly selected users modification permissions.

As the contact data service may provide sensitive private information, such as phone numbers, e-mail addresses, and so on, the HTTP protocol, being a text protocol, may not be secure enough. The information transmitted through it is subject to **man-in-the-middle** attacks, which could lead to data leakage. To prevent such cases, (**Transport Layer Security (TLS)**) should be used. The HTTPS protocol encrypts the transmitted data, ensuring that only appropriate consumers who have the right decryption key will be able to consume the data exposed by the service.

In this chapter, we will be looking at how Node.js enables the following security features:

- Basic authentication
- Passport-based basic authentication
- Passport-based third-party authentication
- Authorization
- Transport Layer Security

Authentication

An application considers a user authenticated when their identity has been successfully validated against a trusted store. Such trusted stores can be either any kind of specially maintained database, storing the credentials of the application (basic authentication), or a third-party service that checks a given identity against its own trusted store (third-party authentication).

Basic authentication

HTTP basic authentication is one of the most popular and straightforward authentication mechanisms available out there. It relies on HTTP headers in the request, which provide the user's credentials. Optionally, the server may reply with a header, forcing the clients to authenticate themselves. The following diagram shows a client-server interaction when basic authentication is carried out:

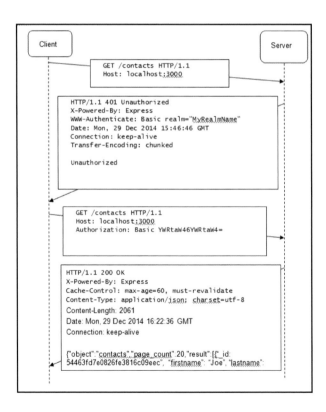

Whenever an HTTP request is sent to an endpoint secured by HTTP basic authentication, the server replies with a HTTP `401 Unauthorized` status code, and optionally with a `WWW-Authenticate` header. This header forces the client to send another request, containing the `Authorization` header, which specifies that the authentication method is `basic`. This request is followed by a base64-encoded key/value pair, providing the username and the password to authenticate with. Optionally, the server can specify a message to the client with the `realm` attribute.

This attributes specifies that resources sharing the same `realm` value should support the same authentication means. In the preceding example, the `realm` message is `MyRealmName`. The client authenticates by sending the `Authentication` header with value `Basic YWRtaW46YWRtaW4`, specifying that `Basic` authentication is used, followed by the base64-encoded value. In the example, the literal `YWRtaW46YWRtaW4` decoded in base64 represents the literal: `admin:admin`. In case such a username-password combination is successfully authenticated, the HTTP server will respond with the JSON payload of the requested contacts. If the authentication fails, the server will respond with the status code `401 Unauthorized`, but this time without including the `WWW-Authenticate` header.

There are several approaches to enable basic authentication in Express applications. Before looking at a few of them, however, we need a data store where the information for our users will be kept:

1. The first step to enable basic authentication would be to define another schema in MongoDB for our authenticated users that should store the login data of the authenticated users:

```
var authUserSchema = new mongoose.Schema({
  username: {type: String, index: {unique: true}},
  password: String,
  role: String,
});

var adminUser = new AuthUser({
  username: 'admin',
  password: 'admin',
  role: 'Admin'
});

adminUser.save(function(error) {
  if (!error) {
    adminUser.save();
    console.log('Creating Admin user');
  } else {
    console.log('Admin user already exist');
```

```
    }
});
```

The schema defines three fields: a unique username, password, and role, which will not be used for now. We will refer to it at a later stage, when providing an authorization concept. This field will specify whether the role assigned to an authenticated user is allowed to carry out data modifications over existing contacts.

Right after the schema definition, our application creates a default admin user. We will use this in the next sample, which demonstrates the basic authentication capability.

2. To enable basic authentication, we will initially use the `basic-auth` Node.js module. It provides an `auth()` function that parses an incoming request, expecting that it contains a valid `Authorization` header for basic authentication with key/value pair with a username bound to the key called `name` and password in the key called `pass`. Let's install the module via the NPM package manager:

   ```
   npm install basic-auth
   ```

3. Next, we will implement a middleware function that makes use of the `WWW-Authenticate` header, as well as a function called `authenticate()` that queries the newly created database using the username and password parsed within the request:

```
app.use(function(request, response, next) {
  var credentials = auth(request);
  if (credentials === undefined) {
      console.log('User information is not available
      in the request');
      response.statusCode = 401;
      response.setHeader('WWW-Authenticate',
      'Basic');
      response.end('Unauthorized');
  } else {
      authenticate(credentials.name,
      credentials.pass, response, next);
  }
});
function authenticate(_username, _password,
response, callback) {
      AuthUser.findOne({username:_username,
      password: _password}, function(error, data) {
            if (error) {
```

```
                console.log('User not found');
                response.statusCode = 401;
                response.end();
                return;
        } else {
                console.log(data.username + '
                authenticated successfully');
                return callback(null,
                data.username);
            }
        }
    });
    }
```

The `authenticate()` function accepts the `next()` function of the middleware in the chain as a parameter and will invoke it if the provided login credentials are found in the authenticated users database. This will cause complete execution of the middleware chain, and finally, the `authenticate()` function will call the route function that provides the result set. If the login is invalid, the `authenticate()` function returns the HTTP 401 `Unauthorized` status code and stops the chain execution, rendering `Unauthorized` to the `response` object.

Passport

There are plenty of authentication methods to choose from nowadays. Perhaps the most popular methods are basic authentication, where each user has their own username and password, and third-party authentication, where users can identify themselves with their own already existing account for an external public service such as personal social services like LinkedIn, Facebook, or Twitter.

Choosing the most appropriate type of authentication for a web API depends mainly on its consumers. Apparently, an application consuming an API to fetch data is not likely to authenticate with a personal social account. This approach is more suitable when the API is used via a frontend directly by a human being.

Implementing a solution capable of switching between different authentication methods easily is a complex and time-consuming task. In fact, it can become hardly possible if not considered at the initial design phase of an application.

Passport is a piece of authentication middleware for Node.js, created especially for use cases where the means of authentication should be easily switched from one to another. It has modular architecture that enables usage of a specific authentication provider, called **strategy**. The strategy takes care of implementing a chosen authentication approach.

There are plenty of authentication strategies to choose from, for example, a regular basic authentication strategy or social-platform-based strategies for services such as Facebook, LinkedIn, Twitter, and so on. Refer to the official Passport website, `http://www.passport js.org/`, for a complete list of available strategies.

Passport's basic authentication strategy

In the *Basic authentication* section, we implemented our own middleware function, which used the `basic-auth` module. Now it is time to see how to utilize Passport's basic authentication strategy:

1. As usual, we will start by installing the relevant modules with the NPM package manager. We will need the `passport` module, which provides the base functionality that allows you to plug in different authentication strategies, and a concrete strategy for basic authentication, provided by the `passport-http` module:

   ```
   npm install passport
   npm install passport-http
   ```

2. Before modifying our application to use Passport authentication middleware, we have to clean it up from the `basic-auth` module. Thus, the `require()` function for that module has to be removed, as well as the `authenticate()` middleware function implemented earlier-we will not be using these anymore. Instead, we will use Passport.

3. First, we have to instantiate both the Passport middleware and the basic authentication strategy. Then, we have to configure them in Express:

   ```
   var passport = require('passport')
     , BasicStrategy = require('passport
     http').BasicStrategy;
   var app = express();
   app.use(passport.initialize());
   ```

   Although the Passport middleware is utilized in the Express application, it is still not used to provide basic authentication for its routes. So, our next step is to pass an instance of the strategy as an argument to the Passport's `use()` function.

4. The `BasicStrategy` option takes a handler function as an argument. It gives us access to the username and password supplied by the client, and to the Passport middleware's `done()` function, which notifies Passport whether the user has been successfully authenticated. Invoke the `done()` function with `user` as an argument in order to grant authenticate or pass the `error` argument to it to revoke the authentication:

```
passport.use(new BasicStrategy(
function(username, password, done) {
  AuthUser.findOne({username: username, password:
  password},
    function(error, user) {
      if (error) {
        console.log(error);
        return done(error);
      } else {
        if (!user) {
          console.log('unknown user');
          return done(error);
        } else {
          console.log(user.username + '
          authenticated successfully');
          return done(null, user);
        }
      }
    });
  })
);
```

5. Finally, use the `authenticate()` function in the router middleware in order to attach it to a specific HTTP method handler function:

```
app.get('/v2/contacts',
cache('minutes',1),
passport.authenticate('basic', { session: false }),
  function(request, response) {
    var get_params = url.parse(request.url,
    true).query;
    if (Object.keys(get_params).length == 0) {
      _v2.paginate(Contact, request, response);
    }
    else {
      if (get_params['limit'] != null ||
      get_params['page'] !=null) {
        _v2.paginate(Contact, request, response);
      }
```

```
            else {
              var key = Object.keys(get_params)[0];
              var value = get_params[key];
              _v2.query_by_arg(Contact, key, value,
              response);
            }
          }
      });
```

The first argument of the `authenticate()` middleware function specifies which strategy should be used to authenticate the request. This provides extra flexibility by enabling us to use different Passport authentication strategies for different HTTP method handlers. The second argument is a set of options that can be passed to Passport.

In our case, we specify that we don't want to store any authentication details in a session. This is because, when using basic authentication, there is no need to store any user information in a session, as each request contains the `Authorization` header that provides the logon details.

Passport's third-party authentication strategies

Today, almost everyone owns at least one personal public social media account such as Twitter, Facebook, LinkedIn, and so on. Recently, it has become really popular for websites to allow their visitors to authenticate themselves via one of their social accounts, by just clicking on an icon will bind their social service account to a service-internal automatically generated account.

This approach is very convenient for web users, who usually are permanently logged in to at least one of their accounts. If they are not currently logged in, clicking on an icon will redirect them to their social service login page, and after a successful login, another redirection takes place, ensuring that the user gets the content they originally requested. When it comes to exposing data via a Web API, this approach is not really an option.

Publicly exposed APIs cannot predict whether they are to be consumed by a human or by an application. Also, APIs aren't usually consumed directly by humans. Thus, third-party authentication is the only option when you, as API authors, are convinced that the exposed data will be available directly to end users who have requested it manually through a frontend from an Internet browser. Once they have successfully logged in to their social account, a unique user identifier will be stored in a session. So, your service will need to be able to handle such sessions appropriately.

To enable session support for storing user login information with Passport and Express, you have to initialize the Express session middleware before initializing Passport and its session middleware:

```
app.use(express.session());
app.use(passport.initialize());
app.use(passport.session());
```

Then, specify the user whose details Passport should serialize/deserialize into or out of the session. For that purpose, Passport provides the `serializeUser()` and `deserializeUser()` functions, which store complete user information in a session:

```
passport.serializeUser(function(user, done) {
  done(null, user);
});

passport.deserializeUser(function(obj, done) {
  done(null, obj);
});
```

 The order of initializing the session handling of the Express and Passport middleware is important. The Express session should be passed to the application first, and should be followed by the Passport session.

After enabling session support, you have to decide which third-party authentication strategy to rely on. Basically, third-party authentication is enabled via a plugin or application created by the third-party provider, for example. a social service site. We will briefly look at creating a LinkedIn application that allows authentication via the OAuth protocol. **OAuth** stands for **OpenAuthorization**. It allows the consumer to identify against a third-party service.

Usually, this is done via a pair of public key and a secret (token) associated with the social media application. Creating a LinkedIn application is easy; you just have to log in to `http://www.linkedin.com/secure/developer` and fill in a brief application information form. You will be given a secret key and a token to enable the authentication. Perform the following steps to enable LinkedIn authentication:

1. Install the `linkedin-strategy` module:

   npm install linkedin-strategy

2. Get an instance of the LinkedIn strategy and initialize it to the Passport middleware by the `use()` function after session support has been enabled:

```
var passport = require('passport')
  , LinkedInStrategy = require('passport-
  linkedin').Strategy;

app.use(express.session());
app.use(passport.initialize());
app.use(passport.session());

passport.serializeUser(function(user, done) {
  done(null, user);
});

passport.deserializeUser(function(obj, done) {
  done(null, obj);
});

passport.use(new LinkedInStrategy({
    consumerKey: 'api-key',
    consumerSecret: 'secret-key',
    callbackURL: "http://localhost:3000/contacts"
  },
    function(token, tokenSecret, profile, done) {
      process.nextTick(function () {
        return done(null, profile);
      });
    })
);
```

3. Specify explicitly that the LinkedIn strategy should be used as Passport for each individual route, ensuring that session handling is enabled:

```
app.get('/v2/contacts',
  cache('minutes',1),
  passport.authenticate('linked', { session: true}),
  function(request, response) {
    //...
  }
});
```

4. Provide a means for a user to log out by exposing a logout URI, making use of `request.logout`:

```
app.get('/logout', function(req, res){
request.logout();
```

```
        response.redirect('/contacts');
    });
```

 The given third-party URLs and service data are subject to change. You should always refer to the service policy when providing third-party authentication.

Authorization

So far, the contacts data service relied on a statically created admin user to access the data. It is time to change that by introducing an API that would provide simple user management capability.

We've already defined AuthUser. Now we will create a module that will take care of creating, updating, and deleting users. The name of the module file will be admin.js, and like the other modules in our application, it will be located in the modules directory:

```
exports.remove = function (model, _username, response) {
  console.log('Deleting user: '+ _username);
  model.findOne({username: _username}, function(error,
  data) {
    if (error) {
      console.log(error);
      if (response != null) {
        response.writeHead(500,
          {'Content-Type' : 'text/plain'});
        response.end('Internal server error');
      }
      return;
    } else {
    if (!data) {
      console.log('User' + _username + ' not found');
      if (response != null) {
        response.writeHead(404,
          {'Content-Type' : 'text/plain'});
        response.end('Not Found');
      }
      return;
    } else {
      data.remove(function(error){
        if (!error) {
          data.remove();
        }
```

```
        else {
          console.log(error);
        }
      });

      if (response != null){
        response.send('Deleted');
      }
      return;
      }
    }
  });
}

exports.update = function (model, requestBody, response) {
  var _username = requestBody.username;
  console.log (requestBody);
  model.findOne({username: _username}, function(error,
  data) {
    if (error) {
      console.log(error);
      if (response != null) {
        response.writeHead(500,
          {'Content-Type' : 'text/plain'});
        response.end('Internal server error');
      }
      return;
      } else {
        var user = toAuthUser(requestBody, model);
        if (!data) {
          console.log('User: ' + _username +
          ' does not exist. It will be created.');
          user.save(function(error) {
            if (!error)
            user.save();
          });

          if (response != null) {
            response.writeHead(201, {'Content-Type' :
            'text/plain'});
            response.end('Created');
          }
          return;
        }

        data.username = user.username;
        data.password = user.password;
        data.role = user.role;
```

```
      data.save(function (error) {
        if (!error) {
          console.log('Successfully updated user: '+
          _username);
          data.save();
        } else {
          console.log('Error on save operation');
        }
      });
      if (response != null) {
        response.send('Updated');
      }
    }
  });
  };


exports.create = function (model, requestBody, response) {
  var user = toAuthUser(requestBody, model);
  var _username = requestBody.username;
  user.save(function(error) {
    if (!error) {
      user.save();
    } else {
      console.log('Checking if user saving failed due to
      already existing user:' + _username);
      model.findOne({username: _username},
function(error, data) {
  if (error) {
    console.log(error);
    if (response != null) {
      response.writeHead(500, {'Content-Type' :
      'text/plain'});
      response.end('Internal server error');
    }
    return;
  } else {
    var user = toAuthUser(requestBody, model);
    if (!data) {
      console.log('The user does not exist. It will be
      created');
      user.save(function(error) {
      if (!error) {
        user.save();
      } else {
        console.log(error);
      }
    });
```

```
      if (response != null) {
        response.writeHead(201, {'Content-Type' :
        'text/plain'});
        response.end('Created');
      }
      return;
    } else {
      console.log('Updating user:' + _username);
      data.username = user.username;
      data.password = user.password;
      data.role = user.role;
      data.save(function (error) {
        if (!error) {
          data.save();
          response.end('Updated');
          console.log('Successfully updated user: ' +
          _username);
        } else {
          console.log('Error while saving user:' +
          _username);
          console.log(error);
        }
      });
    }
  }
});
}
function toAuthUser(body, AuthUser) {
  return new AuthUser({
    username: body.username,
    password: body.password,
    role: body.role
  });
}
```

Now that we have the `admin` module function exported, the next step will be to route it accordingly in our application. We will use the `/admin` URI, similar to the `/contacts` URI. It will be protected by basic authentication by `passport.js`. The administration API, however, needs to be available only for a specific group of users who are actually authorized to manipulate the list of users who have access to the service. To enable authorization, we will use the `role` field of the `AuthUser` schema. Only those users who have an admin role will be allowed to manipulate the user's database.

When Passport's `done()` function is invoked to authenticate a successful login, it takes as a second argument a `model` instance of the user that has been granted authentication. The `done()` function adds that user model instance to the `request` object, and in this way, provides access to it via the `request.user` property after successful authentication. We will make use of that property to implement a function performing the authorization check after successful authentication:

```
function authorize(user, response) {
  if ((user == null) || (user.role != 'Admin')) {
    response.writeHead(403, { 'Content-Type' :
    'text/plain'});
    response.end('Forbidden');
    return;
  }
}
```

 HTTP `403 Forbidden` status code could be easily confused with `405 Not allowed`. However, status code `405 Not Allowed` indicates that a specific HTTP verb is not supported by the requested resource. So, it should be used only in that context.

The `authorize()` function will close the `response` stream, returning status code `403 Forbidden`, which indicates that the logged-in user is recognized but has insufficient permissions. This revokes access to the resource. This function has to be used in each route requiring authorization, that is, each route of the `/admin` URI.

Here is an example of how a `post` route implements authorization:

```
app.post('/admin',
passport.authenticate('basic', { session: false }),
  function(request, response) {
    authorize(request.user, response);
    if (!response.closed) {
      admin.update(AuthUser, request.body, response);
    }
  }
);
```

After `authorize()` is invoked, we check whether the `response` object still allows writing to its output by checking the value of the closed property of the `response` object. It will return `true` once the end function of the `response` object has been called, which is exactly what the `authorize()` function does when the user lacks admin permissions. Thus, we can rely on the closed property in our implementation.

Transport Layer Security

Publicly available information in the web easily becomes the subject of different types of cyber-attacks. Often it is not enough just to keep the so-called "bad guys" out. Sometimes, they won't bother gaining authentication at all and may prefer to carry out a **man-in-the-middle (MiM)** attack, pretending to be the final receiver of a message and sniffing the communication channel that transmits the data—or even worse, altering the data while it flows.

Being a text-based protocol, HTTP transfers data in a human-readable format, which makes it an easy victim of MiM attacks. Unless transferred in an encrypted format, all of the contacts data of our service is vulnerable to MiM attacks. In this section, we will switch our transport from an insecure HTTP protocol to the secure HTTPS protocol.

HTTPS is secured by asymmetric cryptography, also known as **public-key encryption**. It is based on a pair of keys that are mathematically related. The key used for encryption is called **public key**, and the key used for decryption is called **private key**. The idea is to freely provide the encryption key to partners that have to send encrypted messages, and to perform decryption with the private key.

A typical public-key encryption communication scenario between two parties, *A* and *B*, would be the following:

1. Party *A* composes a message, encrypts it with Party *B*'s public key, and sends it.
2. Party *B* decrypts the message with its own private key and processes it.
3. Party *B* composes a response message, encrypts it with Party *A*'s public key, and then sends it.
4. Party *A* decrypts the response message with its own private key.

Now that we know how public-key encryption works, let's go through a sample of HTTPS client-server communication, as shown in this diagram:

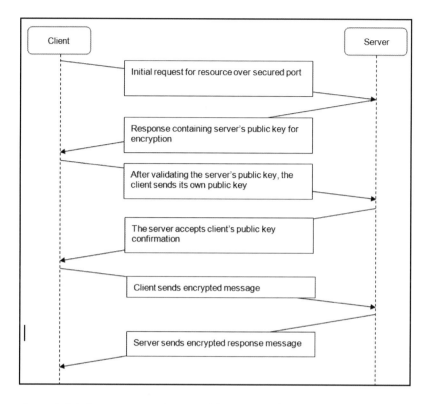

The client sends an initial request against an SSL-secured endpoint. The server responds to that request by sending its public key to be used for encrypting further incoming requests. Then the client has to check the validity and verify the identity of the received key. After successful verification of the server's public key, the client has to send its own public key back to the server. Finally after the key exchange procedure has completed, the two parties can start communicating securely.

HTTPS relies on trust, thus it is vital to have a reliable way of checking whether a specific public key belongs to a specific server. Public keys are exchanged within a X.509 certificate, which has a hierarchical structure. This structure enables clients to check whether a given certificate has been generated from a trusted root certificate. Clients should trust only certificates that have been issued by a known **certificate authority (CA)**.

Before switching our contacts service to use the HTTPS transport, we need a public/private key pair. Since we are not a certificate authority, we will have to use OpenSSL tooling to generate test keys for us.

OpenSSL is available for download at http://www.openssl.org/, where source code distributions are available for all popular operating systems. OpenSSL can be installed as follows:

1. Binary distribution is available for download for Windows, and Debian and Ubuntu users can make use of the packaged distribution by executing the following:

    ```
    sudo apt-get install openssl
    ```

Windows users will have to set an environment variable, OPENSSL_CNF, specifying the location of the openssl.cnf configuration file, typically located in the share directory in the installation archive.

2. Now let's generate a test key/value pair with OpenSSL:

    ```
    opensslreq -x509 -nodes -days 365 -newkey
    rsa:2048-keyoutcontacts.pem -out contacts.crt
    ```

OpenSSL will prompt for some details required for generating the certificate, such as country code, city, fully qualified domain name, and so on. Afterwards, it will generate a private key in the contacts.pem file and a public key certificate that will be valid for a year in the contacts.crt file. We will be using these newly generated files, so copy them in a new subdirectory, called ssl, in the contacts data service directory.

Now we have everything needed to modify our service to use HTTPS:

1. First, we need to switch and use the HTTPS module instead of HTTP and specify the port we want to use to enable HTTPS communication:

    ```
    var https = require('https');
    var app = express();

    app.set('port', process.env.PORT || 3443);
    ```

2. Then, we have to read the private key from the contacts.cem file and the certificate from contacts.crt into an array:

    ```
    var options = {key :
    fs.readFileSync('./ssl/contacts.pem'),
      cert : fs.readFileSync('./ssl/contacts.crt')};
    ```

3. Finally, we pass the array containing the key pair to the HTTPS instance when creating the server, and start listening through the specified port:

```
https.createServer(options,
app).listen(app.get('port'));
```

That's all you need to do to enable HTTPS for an Express-based application. Save your changes and give it a try by requesting `https://localhost:3443/contacts` in a browser. You will be shown a warning message, informing you that the server you are connecting to is using a certificate that is not issued by a trusted certificate authority. That's normal, as we generated the certificate on our own and we are not a CA for sure, so just ignore that warning.

 Before deploying a service on a production environment, you should always ensure that you use a server certificate issued by a trusted CA.

Self-test questions

Go through the following questions:

- Is HTTP basic authentication secure against man-in-the-middle attacks?
- What are the benefits of Transport Layer Security?

Summary

In this chapter, you learned how to protect exposed data by enabling a means of authentication and authorization. This is a critical aspect of any publicly available data service. In addition, you learned how to prevent man-in-the-middle attacks using the secured layer transport protocol between a service and its users. As a developer of such services, you should always consider the most appropriate security features that your application should support.

I hope this was a useful experience! You gained enough knowledge and practical experience, which should have made you much more confident in understanding how RESTful APIs work and how they are designed and developed. I strongly encourage you to go through the code evolution chapter by chapter. You should be able to further refactor it, adopting it to your own coding style. Of course some parts of it could be further optimized, as they repeat quite often. That is an intentional decision rather than good practice, as I wanted to emphasize their importance. You should always strive to improve your codebase, making it easier to maintain.

Finally, I would like to encourage you to always follow the development of the Node.js modules you use in your applications. Node.js has an extraordinary community, eager to grow rapidly. There is always something exciting going on there, so make sure you don't miss it. Good luck!

Index

15067992R00083

Printed in Great Britain
by Amazon